MARRIAGE
BOOT CAMP

MARRIAGE BOOT CAMP

Defeat the Top Ten Marriage Killers and
Build a Rock-Solid Relationship

ELIZABETH AND JIM CARROLL

 New American Library

NEW AMERICAN LIBRARY
Published by New American Library,
an imprint of Penguin Random House LLC
375 Hudson Street, New York, New York 10014

This book is an original publication of New American Library.

First Printing, January 2016

For more information about Penguin Random House, visit penguin.com.

LIBRARY OF CONGRESS CATALOGING-IN-PUBLICATION DATA:
Carroll, Elizabeth, 1956–
Marriage boot camp: defeat the top ten marriage killers and build a rock-solid
relationship/Elizabeth and James Carroll.
p. cm.
ISBN 978-0-451-47677-7 (paperback)
1. Marriage. 2. Marital quality. 3. Married people—Psychology. 4. Interpersonal relations.
5. Interpersonal conflict. I. Carroll, James, 1954– II. Title.
HQ734.C3235 2015
306.81—dc23   2015011862

Printed in the United States of America
10 9 8 7 6 5 4 3 2 1

Designed by Pauline Neuwirth

PUBLISHER'S NOTE
Some names and identifying characteristics have been changed to protect the privacy of
the individuals involved.

Penguin
Random
House

To all the people who serve and volunteer their time and talent to make the original Marriage Boot Camp come to life each and every month.

To our Dallas directors—David and Lisa Bishop, Dana Hamman, Art Stone, Jeff and Tamara Hamner, and Ilsa Norman—who have faithfully served the Marriage Boot Camp for decades.

To our Houston and Atlanta directors—Cliff and Jeani Poe, Todd and Teresa Hicks, and Angie and Tony Craft—who each share our passion for creating healthy, happy marriages.

To our amazing production team at Thinkfactory Media, headed by Adam Freeman, who have taken our original Marriage Boot Camp ministry and brought it to life for the TV audience.

To our WE tv partners—Suzanne Murch, Lauren Gellert, Marc Juris, and their teams—for believing in the vision of Marriage Boot Camp.

CONTENTS

· · · · · · · · · · · · · · · · · · · ·

MARRIAGE
BOOT CAMP

WELCOME TO MARRIAGE BOOT CAMP!

HAVE YOU BEEN A fan of the *Marriage Boot Camp* television series on WE tv? Some of you may have seen every season; the first two seasons consisted of participants from the infamous *Bridezillas* television show, followed by several seasons of reality stars from various television shows and genres. We've found that putting a mix of all different varieties of couples together in a boot-camp environment is helpful; not only will couples see the snarls and tangles in their own marriages, but seeing the struggles of other couples helps them in their own lives.

While these men and women come from varied socioeconomic backgrounds, educations, and places, they all came into the Marriage Boot Camp program struggling with equally daunting marital problems.

Our Bridezillas were really fascinating. We repeatedly heard from fans of the show that nobody was surprised to find those women having trouble in their relationships; it was what they expected after watching how they behaved toward their future spouses during their wedding planning and on the big day.

But through *Marriage Boot Camp*, we saw what was behind the tantrums portrayed on their shows and how in some cases, their future spouses had a lot to do with triggering their behavior. We saw the pain couples suffer when one or both of them are dishonest and hiding things. All of them finished our program more aware of their spouse's needs and more understanding of the kind of respect and trust a marriage requires. Some of these women were less Bridezilla divas and more legitimately concerned wives. Really, in today's world, if you cannot allow your spouse to look at your cell phone, there are much deeper trust issues that need serious consideration.

What many viewers don't know is that Marriage Boot Camp existed long before the television show first aired in May of 2013. We created Marriage Boot Camp workshops and counseling seminars almost twelve years before we began appearing on television to share our approach to strengthening a marriage. To date more than ten thousand couples have participated in our workshops, and we commissioned a two-year study in 2001 that demonstrated *exactly* how successful the Marriage Boot Camp protocol is.

Statistically, traditional marriage counseling works only twenty percent of the time. Our study proved that *eighty* percent of the couples who used Marriage Boot Camp for relationship counseling went on to have happy and successful marriages. There's nothing else like it—no other therapy program can claim a success rate that high.

Why is Marriage Boot Camp so successful? Because it forces struggling couples to step back and reevaluate everything, which includes looking in the mirror at their own issues. We often say that we have to take the marriage apart and look at every component to get to the root of the problem so we can build the marriage back up and give it a chance to work. Our program forces both spouses to not only hear and learn more about the needs and desires and fears of their partners, but we also put them in situations where they actually experience what their spouse is feeling for themselves.

HOW WILL THIS BOOK WORK FOR YOU?

You've picked up this book because you're struggling in your own relationship and you're wondering if reading this will help. Or you're a massive fan of the show, in which case you'll also enjoy reading about the process and gaining more understanding about what you're seeing on television. The original Marriage Boot Camp seminar program tools are what you're seeing on WE tv's reality show, but the show gives us the ability to more graphically and vividly let the campers experience certain aspects of drills that couldn't be executed in a classroom. The book breaks the program down into the steps we use to get these couples from a dark place to an enlightened understanding of each other's needs and wants. And eighty percent of the time, it's been proven to work to save a relationship in distress.

The foundation for this book comes from the Marriage Boot Camp seminar series and WE tv's reality television show. We've taken many of the games, drills, and exercises we teach and put them in a readable, functional format to bring you an experience of healing that you can do at home. The chapters contain some guided visualizations that drop the reader into the world of the imagination to consider life from a different perspective. Stories and anecdotes from those who have already gone through the Marriage Boot Camp will illustrate how others have applied our teachings to their own lives. Then we give you several exercises that apply topic-specific activities to your life. By the time you've finished the book, you will have tools for living life and experiencing relationships more fully and more effectively. While there are many things that can negatively impact your marriage, after close to twenty years of shepherding spouses toward their own happily ever after, we have boiled this book down to the top-ten marriage killers: communication problems, sex problems, money disagreements, battling over chores, personality differences, parenting challenges, cheating, inability to resolve conflict, refusing to let go of the past, and issues surrounding the need for forgiveness.

If you can master these areas of challenge, then you, too, may find purpose in spreading the word: You can have the marriage you've always wanted!

WHY IS MARRIAGE SO HARD?

We all desperately long for a happy relationship. We were born into relationships, helpless and vulnerable, and had it not been for relationships, we would have perished. Not much has changed except the fact that we can physically survive, but a part of us dies without an intimate connection.

We are created to love and be loved, and there is no greater opportunity for this love than in marriage. We are called to become one with another so that we can touch each other's deepest needs: the need for security—knowing that we are loved—and the need for significance—knowing that we are valued. So why is marriage so hard? It is hard because in order to be successful in marriage, *you* have to be solid and whole. That means you have to love yourself, delight in the unique creation of you, and appreciate the unique creation reflected in others. You have to be able to love yourself before you can love anyone else . . . yet marriage will not tolerate selfishness.

The dissolution of marriage through divorce has become commonplace and widespread, with a marriage success rate hovering around fifty percent in the United States. If a disease affected more than half of the populace, spreading suffering to all age groups, we would frantically search for a solution, but the disease of divorce is virtually ignored. Politicians may talk about returning to family values, and current events may inspire discussions of how the dissolution of the family unit has caused the havoc going on in some cities, but at the end of the day, nobody is doing anything about it. It's all rhetoric.

Well, not anymore. This book takes on the divorce disease and more. It will help you understand who you are, why you are the way you are, and how these traits result in the marriage that you have. Once you understand the reasons that your life is the way it is today, we give you the tools to choose different beliefs and actions to get to a different outcome. The result is the marriage that you've always wanted.

Maybe you're reading this book because you're struggling with your relationship but your partner isn't willing to embark on counseling together. That's okay. You can start this program alone. Our hope is that once you've read the book, you'll be better able to communicate with your partner based on the exercises and tools we've provided you.

However, it's worth the struggle to ask your spouse to work the

Marriage Boot Camp program with you and try to make progress in your lives together. Even if he or she isn't ready to tackle the whole enchilada with you at one time, you may be able to navigate *some* of the steps and drills together without making your partner feel tested or judged. You may even find him or her more amenable than you thought! So be prepared just in case your spouse says yes when you initiate the discussion; some of the exercises are fun but require a little prep work for the uninitiated.

WHAT KIND OF "REAL" COUPLES DO THE MARRIAGE BOOT CAMP?

All kinds of couples participate in Marriage Boot Camp. Fans of the show know that the backgrounds and relationship problems of the couples all vary dramatically. Every human being is different, and each of us processes our relationships differently.

Here's a little snapshot of a real (as in non-reality-television) couple who attended our active, experiential seminar:

It is ten o'clock on a Wednesday morning and forty couples enter the Marriage Boot Camp room. There's a crackle in the air, but it is not the crackle of excitement. It is the crackle of pain. All of the couples are here because their marriages are in trouble. Many of them don't want to be here but have come because they deeply love their spouse despite their relationship problems and they want to try to fix their marriages. For more than half of the couples in the room, this is their last-ditch effort to save their marriage. Many have already filed for divorce. We also have pre-marrieds doing the hard work before the wedding. Smart.

Some of the people in the room are here because they were dragged, coerced by their spouse, family, friends, or children to try one more thing before ending their marriage. Most of the people in the room are desperate for help even if attending Marriage Boot Camp wasn't their idea.

Take the example of Bobby and Melissa:

Bobby and Melissa have been married for six years. They have two children, ages six and three. At nineteen years old, they found themselves accidentally pregnant and unmarried. Their dreams of education and individual successes were dashed in that instant. Bobby carries a deep-seated resentment toward Melissa, feeling that she manipulated him by getting pregnant. Melissa feels unfairly accused because the pregnancy was as much Bobby's fault as hers. They ended their relationship during the pregnancy, dated other people, but kept coming back together out of their love for their son and a powerful sexual attraction. When Bobby decided to enter the military, he found that his benefits would be much greater if he were married. Plus, he didn't want to travel the world alone. So for all the wrong reasons, Bobby and Melissa got married.

They tried to do marriage right, even having a second child together, but over time infidelity, deception, and lengthy absences poisoned whatever love they felt for each other. Both of them wanted to have a happy marriage, but they also both realized they didn't know how to achieve that goal. They read every self-help book they could find and also participated in marriage counseling. Coming to Marriage Boot Camp was their last-ditch effort to avoid divorce.

Bobby and Melissa both grew up in dysfunctional homes with revolving father figures. Neither had ever seen a truly healthy, loving marriage, and they were well on the road to giving their children the same dysfunctional home that they had grown up in—the last thing they wanted to do. Their primary motivation for working out their relationship lay in the fact that they didn't want to see their children suffer the way they had.

Upon arrival, Bobby and Melissa were both challenged to give one hundred percent to the Marriage Boot Camp program. They were promised they would be given the tools to have a healthy, happy, fulfilling marriage. But they were also warned that just having the tools wouldn't be enough to save their marriage. We asked this question: "Do you want to grow and heal and learn so that you can have a healthy marriage, or do you want to drag all of your dysfunction from this marriage into your future?"

Bobby and Melissa committed to giving one hundred percent. Both had little hope that their marriage would survive (some couples who travel to attend our boot camps actually arrive dreading spending even a few days in their hotel room together, much less contemplate spending the next ten, twenty, or forty years together), but they knew that they would have to co-parent their two small children whether or not they remained married. They both knew firsthand what it was like to have parents who couldn't work together and who made life miserable for the children, and neither wanted to be *that* parent.

It was a difficult seminar for them, but the end result is that Bobby and Melissa were able to forgive each other, and themselves, for past transgressions and move forward. They learned how to communicate their needs and fears in a healthier manner. Marriages are never perfect, and they all require work and attention, but for now Bobby and Melissa both feel more safe and secure and able to provide the kind of family life for their children that they themselves had craved.

WHAT'S THE NEXT STEP?

You, too, can be "happily married," but you have to be willing to give one hundred percent, dig deep, and work your butt off. This book will take you through the process of Marriage Boot Camp, and if you are indeed giving it your all, you'll be pushed, prodded, and guided to become the best possible version of yourself. It is our experience that if you grow, your marriage will grow and you can have the marriage you've always wanted.

1

COMMUNICATION

WITH GOOD COMMUNICATION SKILLS, you can solve virtually any problem. With bad communication skills, you will struggle to solve even the smallest issues. We're going to show you how to breathe new life into your relationship, and love into your hearts, through skillful communication.

> Com·mu·ni·ca·tion *noun* \kə-ˌmyü-nə-ˈkā-shən\: the act or process of using words, sounds, signs, or behaviors to express or exchange information or to express your ideas, thoughts, feelings, etc., to someone else.

According to the *Merriam-Webster Dictionary*, the definition of "communication" is pretty straightforward. Why is this the biggest problem in relationships? Because it's not just the act of communicating; it's also the manner in which you communicate. Is what you're saying what is really true for you? Did you convey the message you intended? Good communication requires self-awareness and the courage to share your inner life with another person.

Communication is the bridge between two people. It takes our ideas, thoughts, and feelings from inside our heads and presents them as a gift to the listener, in this case, someone you care about. Communication is the solution to the problem of guessing what's going on in each other's heads. Communicating with your partner tells him or her, "I realize that you cannot read my mind."

Many of our problems in life come from the mistaken idea that everybody sees things the same way that we do. Communication is the solution to what psychologists call the "egocentric predicament." It gives each half of a couple the opportunity to check in with their mate to see if their perspective makes sense to at least one other person.

Talking through our thought life is also important because it allows our ideas to take shape and gain clarity and precision. Sometimes our initial ideas are just undeveloped seeds, and communication is the soil in which those ideas blossom.

 **QUICK QUIZ**

Ask yourself the following questions: Do you sometimes feel that you have no idea what your mate is talking about? Do you and your mate fight because each of you heard something completely different from what was intended? Do you feel like you're not completely *heard* by your mate? Does your mate try to fix you or your problem but succeed only in frustrating you further? Have you failed to take the time to let your mate know what you really want from him or her?

It may come as a surprise to you that these are common struggles that every couple grapples with in marriage. Communication is complex and involves a unique personal language for every individual. For really strong communication, you have to be multilingual. Not only do you have to be able to speak your own unique and personal language fluently, but you also have to be able to hear and interpret every other person's unique and personal language. This can be especially difficult with someone you love.

And guess what? Language by itself is inadequate. The words we speak are only a small part of the message that gets transmitted. Research shows that eighty percent of the meaning of a given communication is telegraphed nonverbally. In other words, your body language and facial expressions are extremely important in communicating your feelings. That's why communicating by phone, text, or e-mail can go so far sideways. One couple came in distraught over this text: "YOU DIDN'T GET IT!"

He had made the unforgivable error of inadvertently leaving caps lock on and didn't realize he was yelling at his wife. She had completely overlooked the attached photo of her husband holding her strep results with a big smile on his face.

Do the complexities of communication sound overwhelming? After years of fine-tuning strategies at the Marriage Boot Camp, we are here to help you with some very simple tools to improve the way you communicate with your life partner.

Let's jump into the topic of communication with a discussion of language and ask an important question: **What's more important in communication, logic or emotion?**

We at the Marriage Boot Camp can tell you from experience (including our own experience!) that *both* logic and emotion are important in communication. In fact, they represent two distinct languages that you must fluently speak if you want to have a healthy, happy relationship. We all speak two languages: an emotional language and a logical language. The logical language is easy; it is the sharing of information. The emotional language is a bit more complicated in that it is typically indirect and we are sharing our feelings, our hearts.

Emotional language is asking for *affirmation*, not *information*. On an emotional level, we want to hear that we are valued, loved, and competent, although we are often indirect in how we ask that question of our mate. We all speak an emotional language but often don't realize it. You've heard about people speaking with their hearts instead of their heads; this is what they're talking about.

> Emotional language is asking for *affirmation*, not *information*.

Our emotional language is also a call for connection. When a woman says, "Do I look fat in this dress?" what she's really saying is "Pay attention to how I look and affirm that you find me attractive." Men speak an emotional language as well, but in our culture we often teach them to ignore this language altogether. Make no mistake, though; both men and women make bids to connect. It just may look very different.

Connection is often indirect. Putting our hearts out there makes us vulnerable and at risk of being hurt. If we took the emotional language and made it direct instead of indirect, we might be saying things like:

- I need to feel close to you right now.
- I want to feel like we belong together.
- I want to know that you love me.
- I need to feel attractive to you.
- I want your attention and I want to feel important.
- I want to feel that you delight in me.
- I want to be with you, not alone.
- I want you to make me feel important.

The problem occurs when you are using logic and your mate is using emotion, or vice versa. It's almost like having two completely different conversations on the same topic.

One of the keys to healthy communication is knowing how and when to use logical language versus emotional language. Not only do you have to learn to speak both languages, but you also need to be able to recognize which language your mate is speaking, so you can answer in the same language. And don't get caught up in the notion that speaking an emotional language is the same as lying—it's not. It's simply answering the *real* question under the surface words.

So what exactly does emotional language look like? Well, here's an example of an emotional question that we struggled with while we were developing this theory.

Elizabeth's Story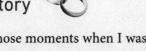

It was one of those moments when I was feeling insecure. So what better way to get rid of this feeling of insecurity than to ask my beloved husband, Jim, a simple question: "Have you ever had great sex with anyone other than me?" Now, keep in mind that Jim has been very grateful, positive, and affirming about our sex life in the past, so I thought this question was kind of a no-brainer. I did not expect (or like) the answer I got. He replied: "Of course. I mean, I've had orgasms before."

For those of you cringing, you understand my pain. For those of you shrugging and saying "What's the problem with that answer?" please read on and let me help you understand the difference between emotional language and logical language.

Take the commonly asked question of wife to husband prior to heading out the door to an important event: "Does my butt look fat in this dress?"

If you are *Star Trek*'s Mr. Spock and you answer this question from a purely logical standpoint, you might say: "Yes. Your butt looks fat in everything. That's because butts are made of fat. The fat is there to cushion you when you sit." Oh jeez. Clearly, a husband like that doesn't understand what his wife is asking.

A clearer way to ask that same question would be more along the lines of: "Do you love me even when I'm not feeling good about my body?" or "I'm feeling self-conscious about my weight; I really need some encouragement or positive feedback!" But few of us ever ask a body-image question that way. So frequently, a logically responding husband gets himself into trouble when he meant no harm at all; he just didn't pick up his wife's emotional cues.

Maybe some of you truly want a logic-based response to this question. Context often determines the proper response. Compare the same question asked in different venues. Asked on the dance floor at a formal affair, you're looking for an emotional answer. You want to hear that your butt looks amazing in the dress. But in the dressing room at Macy's while choosing that dress for the event, you would probably be looking for a more straightforward and logical answer.

The same disconnect would take place if you answered a logical question with an emotional answer. For example, if your husband asks, "Where are my keys?" and you give him an emotional answer like "I know you love your car," your partner may look at you like you've lost your mind. In other words, you must understand the question through a filter of context, love, respect, and compassion. Choose wrong and give a logical answer to an emotional question, or vice versa, and the fight is on.

DOUBLE JEOPARDY

Okay, so what happens if the other person follows up with another potentially emotional question masked in logic? What if a husband answers, "You look great in everything," and she replies, "You're full of crap. I know you're lying. Just tell me the truth!" When this happens, she is probably looking for a specific affirmation, and you should pick up on her cue and continue to respond emotionally. Reaffirm what you said and be specific in your observation. You might say, "Actually, your legs look really long in that," or, "I like that even more than your pink dress," which she knows you love. If she continues to question you, ask for clarification. "What do you think doesn't look good about the dress? I think it looks great on you." If she gets specific, you can respond and make her feel more secure. "No, your butt doesn't look fat, but your cleavage looks fantastic." Boom! That will make her smile. Bottom line: Don't take the bait. Always err on the side of love when asked an emotional question!

Here are some typical emotional questions from the ladies:

- Do I look fat?
- Would you marry me all over again?
- Do I look as good as when we first met?
- What would happen if we met each other for the first time right now?
- Was sex ever great with anyone else?
- Can you imagine being with anyone else?

Men are less obvious with their emotional language, and their needs are frequently about respect. Men will often brag, tell sports stories, complain about the bills, or moan about how hard they work. It is your job to pay attention to your mate's emotional language and be prepared to give affirmation when it is needed.

For example, men might say:

- Do you remember when I . . . ?
- I am swamped at work . . .
- Traffic is a nightmare . . .

BOOT CAMP CALL TO ACTION

Think about your own emotional language. What things do you say that could be misinterpreted as a logical question when you are really asking for affirmation, not information? Hint: These are things you usually say right before a fight! Write down your personal examples. What would you love to hear? What do you need to hear? Write out the perfect response to your emotional language and be prepared to share this with your mate.

MARRIAGE BOOT CAMP QUICK SCRIPT

Since not all of us have a natural ability to respond emotionally, with affirmation instead of information, we recommend you use the "Marriage Boot Camp Quick Script" to give you a model of how to respond if your mate says one of the following:

Do I look fat? This is not a time for a critique of how many pounds she/he needs to lose. "You look beautiful! When I look at you I see . . ." (Fill in the blank with every wonderful thing you observe; start from the top and work your way down. For example, shiny, gorgeous, healthy hair, glowing skin, beautiful breasts, a tiny waist, sexy round hips, and long legs.) "I do not see fat. Are you unhappy with your weight? I'm not."

Would you marry me all over again? Do not say no unless you want your marriage to end. Think about the person that you wanted for your mate and speak from that place. "Of course I would! You are my soul mate, my best friend, and the love of my life. You are the person who shares everything with me."

Do I look as good as when we first met? "No, you look better. Our life together is written all over you, and it adds beauty and depth."

What would happen if we met each other for the first time right now? "I would feel the same magic that I felt the first time— even more intensely than when we met."

Was sex ever great with anyone else? "The combination of the words 'sex' and 'great' only happens when we are together. You are wonderful. I can't even compare it to anyone else I've been with because you're the only one who has ever mattered this much."

Can you imagine being with anyone else? "I can't imagine being with anyone but you."

Do you remember when I . . . ? "I do! But tell me again. I love that story." This also presents a wonderful opportunity in a social setting for you to say, "Honey, tell that story about . . ." and encourage your mate to relive the happy moments.

I am swamped at work . . . "You work so hard and I'm grateful for everything you do for us. You're so good at what you do, and I'm really proud of you."

Traffic is a nightmare . . . "And you make this drive every day. Thank you for your sacrifice and how hard you work for us."

Sam and Nancy's Story

When Sam and Nancy came to the Marriage Boot Camp, they said their biggest problem was communication, but when we went through the discussion of emotional versus logical language, Nancy didn't believe it applied to them. Asked to describe one of their fights, Nancy said, "That's easy! Just yesterday Sam and I got into a big fight because he always ignores me and is on his computer all the time."

Sam explained that he works from home and his work requires him to be on his computer. "It's my *job*. Nancy criticizes me about being on the computer, but she doesn't complain when my paycheck comes." I asked them to describe exactly how the fight started, and Sam said, "Nancy just started bitching at me, and I blew up."

I asked, "What exactly did Nancy say?"

Nancy jumped in and said, "I walked into his office and, real sweet-like, I said, 'Whatcha doin'?' The next thing I know, he's yelling at me and saying, 'I'm working! What does it look like?'"

So I asked Nancy, "When you say, 'Whatcha doin'?' in that sweet, childlike voice, what does that mean?" Nancy thought for a moment, then said, "I guess it means that I want him to spend time with me, but instead he blows up at me and I feel like he just hates me."

Then I asked Sam what *he* thought she meant when she said, "Whatcha doin'?" He responded, "I feel like she's questioning my work ethic and time management." Eventually they were able to see how Nancy uses an emotional language when she says "Whatcha doin'?" and she wants an emotional response of affirmation like "Nothing that is more important than you! What's up?" This was a huge lightbulb moment for both of them, and they were able to see how they were missing each other's emotional communication, leading to unnecessary conflict.

Practicing Communication

We recommend a technique called "the interview." You'll simply ask your mate to tell you something about themselves. And, let's face it, everyone loves it when you show interest in them; this isn't something that changes over time. Sometimes, when we've been coupled for a long time, we forget about what kind of attention our partner needs.

First tee up the subject by describing the difference between an emotional language and a logical language and give examples of each. Then ask your mate to give you an example of a way they've communicated a need for affirmation that may have looked like a request for information. (Be prepared to share your emotional language and what it looks like and what kind of response you would really like.) Then ask your mate how it would make them feel if you were to respond to their emotional language in the way they want. Once a couple becomes "bilingual" in their relationship, many conflicts can simply be avoided.

THE ABCS OF MARRIAGE BOOT CAMP

As we have learned, communication is complicated! Not only do you have to be multilingual, but you have to know what language you are speaking, when you are speaking it, and what language your mate is speaking and when. Whew! In an attempt to simplify communication, Marriage Boot Camp breaks every situation down into the ABCs—action, belief, and consequence.

Before we go deeper into the explanation, take a moment and imagine that you are sitting in a room full of people. Jim and I walk in, and before we say a word to you, we grab a bucketful of Nerf balls and start pelting everyone with them. What would you be thinking? How would you feel? What would you think about doing in response? What about your mate? What would he or she do? Whenever we do this drill, we get a litany of responses from: "You guys are trying to wake us up," to "This is a game; this is fun." Sometimes we hear, "You guys are attacking us." So here is the ABC: The action is Jim and me throwing Nerf balls at everyone; the belief depends on your perspective; the consequence is how this makes you feel, which depends on your belief, and that could be anything!

Kathy and Gary's Story

Kathy was furious with Gary. She said Gary is sneaky and she doesn't feel that she can trust him. Gary spent seven hundred dollars for an expensive gym membership and didn't tell Kathy about it; she only found out about it when she was looking through their credit-card statement. In the past, they'd always discussed large purchases together before spending the money. Compounding the situation, Kathy's mother had just had surgery and was staying with them while she recovered. Between caring for her mother and caring for their three small children, Kathy's home life was pretty challenging. She was feeling exhausted, unattractive, and miserable. The fight erupted one morning when Kathy awoke to find that Gary was gone. When she finally got ahold of him, the first thing she said to him was, "WE ARE DONE!"

Not surprisingly, Gary viewed the situation differently. He felt they could afford the gym membership and that Kathy was being irrational to object. She was simply begrudging him the time to work out.

Understanding how each of them interpreted the situation was the first step in unraveling this communication conflict.

At Marriage Boot Camp, we use the ABCs to break down communication into its three component parts. Pay very careful attention to this section (and maybe even flag these pages), because we will refer to it frequently in the following chapters and you will need to work the steps repeatedly.

THE ABC FORMULA

A = ACTION—Every situation begins with an action.

B = BELIEF—Every action elicits a belief about the action.

C = CONSEQUENCE—Based on the belief, a consequence, or feeling, follows.

To test this theory, I'd like you and your mate to take a look at this picture and, separately, describe the **ACTION** and the **BELIEF** as you see it. Then discuss the **CONSEQUENCE**—how this situation makes you feel, from your perspective—and what you think will happen next.

You may have said something like:

ACTION—She's talking on the phone.

BELIEF—He believes that she's wasting time gossiping with her girlfriends.

CONSEQUENCE—He feels angry and accuses her of wasting time, and that starts a fight.

You could also have said something like:

ACTION—She's on the phone at work.

BELIEF—He believes that she's hard at work providing for her family.

CONSEQUENCE—He feels good about her, and this goodwill flavors their home.

The point of the illustration above is that two people often see the same action but interpret it very differently. Based on how you understand it, the consequence can be a disruption of the connection you feel with your mate, and that can lead to conflict.

Personal Beliefs Are Not Universal Beliefs

In the case of Gary and Kathy, they had very different beliefs about the exact same action.

ACTION—Gary goes to the gym and is gone when Kathy wakes up.

BELIEF—Gary believes that going to the gym is something that he is entitled to do and it's good for him and for his family. When Gary goes to the gym, it relaxes him and makes him perform better at work, which makes him a better provider for his family.

Kathy's perspective, or **BELIEF**, is that Gary goes to the gym to avoid her and the kids and to flirt with the female trainers. She thinks Gary is sneaky. The **CONSEQUENCE** of their difference in perspectives is conflict. Gary feels that the only way he can take care of himself is to sneak around and hide from Kathy. Kathy feels neglected and unloved and, in her anger, lashes out at Gary, confirming Gary's belief. The fact that Gary kept the gym membership a secret confirms Kathy's belief that she cannot trust him.

BOOT CAMP CALL TO ACTION

ABC Conflict Diagram

We are now going to focus on *one* issue that creates conflict in your relationship. Make sure that you pick an issue that is small, so that you can stay focused on learning how to communicate. Let's take this issue and diagram it out like you would diagram a sentence. We are *not* going to try to solve this issue right now; that comes later. You will label the:

A = ACTION—What is the **ACTION** that starts the conflict?

B = BELIEF—What do you **BELIEVE** this action means? This will be very personal and will most likely be different from your mate's belief about the **ACTION**.

C = CONSEQUENCE—How do you feel about this, and what happens next?

Getting your mate involved in this exercise is the ideal scenario, but if you cannot, try to put yourself in your mate's shoes and do your best to answer for him or her. Here are a few examples of common conflict topics: money, sex, disciplining the children, friendships outside the marriage, time management, electronics, being on time, family time.

Use whatever illustration style you want—write it, draw it, chart it, or whatever—just be sure to label it according to the ABC designations. Here's an example:

Partner 1:

(A) When you come home late from work, (B) I believe that you are procrastinating because you don't want to spend time with me, and then (C) I feel hurt and angry and give you the cold shoulder when you walk in the door.

Partner 2:

(A) When I come home late from work, (B) I believe that it's no big deal because I work hard to provide for my family, and then (C) I feel good about myself and expect appreciation, not a fight.

Engaging Your Mate

In Marriage Boot Camp, we often see one partner wanting to work on the relationship and one partner who is reticent to engage. Frequently, one partner simply does not want to fight and avoids engagement. If that describes your situation, here are some suggestions for starting a conversation with your mate:

- First, do a "heart check." Be sure that your reason for wanting to engage is about enhancing your relationship and growing personally. If your motivation is the desire to be right, to punish your mate, or to win an argument, you're setting your marriage up to fail.
- Second, tee up the conversation with an affirmation. Tell your mate you've been reading a book about marriage out of a desire to be closer, that you love him or her, and that you want to be the best possible mate that you can be.

■ Third, get specific. Tell your mate that you found a quick exercise that might help clear up some miscommunication. Tell them that you diagrammed out the ABCs of "blank" (and fill in the blank with a description of the issue at hand) and that it helped you see his or her side of the issue a little more clearly. Say you tried to put yourself in their shoes to see it from his or her point of view, as per the instructions in the book, and now you want to check in to see if you're on target. That should start the dialogue.

■ Finally, if you have been successful in engaging your partner, share your diagrams with each other. If you're still flying solo at this point, continue reading this next section because it will give you a very important tool for communication.

Couples Application

Once you and your partner have written out your ABC diagrams, you are going to share them, which is the first step toward healthy communication. Take turns sharing and listening. When you are the listener, don't comment, but pay very close attention to what your partner says, because you will be asked to comment on it later.

MIRRORING

Before we go any further, let's tackle a new skill. This is very important, and it's a skill you'll be asked to use repeatedly as we work our way through the Marriage Boot Camp program. If you can master "mirroring," it will revolutionize your communication. Mirroring, or reflective listening, is a communication tool that involves two key steps. First you work to listen carefully to understand the speaker's idea, and then you mirror back what you heard to confirm to the speaker that you heard them correctly. Empathic connection, not accurate parroting of information, is at the center of this tool. Psychologist Carl Rogers first coined this concept in his theory of client-centered therapy, and it attempts to "reconstruct what the client is thinking and feeling and to relay this understanding back to the client." All trained therapists go through intense training on this one skill.

When you mirror, you are momentarily putting your own feelings and opinions on hold. Your focus turns to the *other* person's feelings and opinions, and you will consider them *without judgment*. You are not being asked to agree or support their position. You are simply being asked to see their position. This is harder than it seems, but let's take a shot, using an easy-to-solve example.

YOU: Share your ABC conflict with your partner. Keep your description short and concise; don't talk for more than two minutes. Be sure to communicate your feelings as clearly as possible.

YOUR PARTNER: Mirror your mate. Say, "What I heard you say is . . ." (describe for no more than one minute).

STOP. DO NOT DISCUSS THE ISSUE YET.

YOUR PARTNER: Share your ABC conflict with your partner. Keep your description short and concise and stay within the allotted time (two minutes).

YOU: Mirror your mate. Start off by saying, "What I heard you say is . . ." (one minute).

STOP. DO NOT DISCUSS THE ISSUE YET.

For many couples, this would be a perfect time for a fight—which is why we asked you to start with something small. Share, mirror, then STOP! Hearing the difference in perspective can make you want to defend your position, which is exactly what you want to avoid. Stay focused on how your mate feels about the issue and realize that your partner's point of view is different because he or she is different.

Not only will you be tempted to defend your position, but it could also make you want to challenge the speaker or try to rewrite the story with more "accuracy." For now we ask that you hold your thoughts and feelings about this conflict in check until we give you more of the Marriage Boot Camp tools for conflict resolution.

Here's what the exercise looked like for Kathy and Gary:

Kathy's perspective
(A) When Gary goes to the gym, (B) Kathy believes that Gary is sneaky and he is avoiding her and the kids because he doesn't want to spend time with the family, and (C) she feels hurt and angry, then blows up at Gary and says something ugly (we call this "trigger talk," but more on that later) and Gary goes further into his cave to hide.

Gary's perspective
(A) When Gary goes to the gym, (B) Gary believes that he is getting some badly needed "me time," which helps him relax and get his life in perspective, and (C) Gary feels guilty but entitled at the same time, so when Kathy blows up at Gary and says something ugly and Gary goes further into his cave to hide, it confirms his belief that the only way he can get "me time" is to be sneaky about it.

This was the beginning of Kathy and Gary's journey, and the first step was for them to recognize the difference in their "Bs," how their beliefs made them feel and how this was a roadblock on the path to reconnecting.

The point of the ABC drill is to answer two questions:

1. Does your belief match your mate's? As we've discussed, probably not, but we have to do some digging to be sure. Our beliefs are buried just beneath our conscious awareness, where they give meaning and structure to our outer world. But just like a computer's operating system, they are invisible unless there is a problem. We often don't realize that they are even there!

2. Does your belief work *for* your relationship or *against* your relationship?

Our beliefs (you might think of them as "assumptions") are bubbling away beneath the surface, silently affecting and directing our thoughts, and most of the time this system works well. Our beliefs help us make sense of the world, pursue our goals, and even make us attractive to our mates. But some of our beliefs include distorted or erroneous information and spur us to thoughts or conclusions that are unhelpful at best and destructive at worst. We have to bring those beliefs to conscious awareness and recognize that they are creating *feelings we do not need to feel*.

The good news is that you have choices in your thought life, that thoughts do not arise out of nowhere and are not uncontrollable. Unfortunately, feelings are another matter. You cannot *will* yourself to feel differently, even when someone says, "You shouldn't feel that way." Have you ever noticed how annoying it is to hear those words? We intuitively know that we cannot flip our feelings on and off like a light switch. But feelings are clues that should lead us back to our thoughts. Ask yourself, "What was I thinking (the "B") right before I got angry (the "C")?" This is a key element in healthy communication and the point of the ABC exercise.

Mindfulness is the practice of thinking about our thoughts, of slowing down long enough to savor and contemplate the activities of our own minds, and choosing which thoughts to keep and which ones to discard. It's about perspective. We can choose to see the glass half full or half empty, just as we can see the balls as toys or weapons, and this will affect the way we feel.

In one of our recent boot camps, there was a young man who was resistant to virtually every exercise. He joked and fooled around, and everyone started to become annoyed with him. The anger that he inspired in the group caused us to ask him to share about his life. From this discussion, the group got to know him on a deeper level, and he trusted us enough to share a tragic childhood experience that caused him to put on this tough, funny shell. Once we understood this additional facet of his life, not only did we stop seeing him as annoying, but we ended up loving him because our "B" about him changed.

Not only is it important to understand each other's ABCs, but we also have to understand how to make each other feel loved. Before Marriage Boot Camp could help Gary and Kathy resolve their conflict, we first had to build a foundation; they needed to be clear on what they wanted from each other. Understanding what your spouse wants from you and what you want from your spouse is an important starting point for any couple. This next section will help you get a better understanding of how to meet each other's needs.

Love Dots

This game is based on the book *The Five Love Languages: How to Express Heartfelt Commitment to Your Mate* by Gary Chapman. This book posits that there are five different "love languages" and that each of us feels most loved when our mate is speaking our particular love language. One thing we have learned in the Marriage Boot Camp: We all love *all* of the different love languages. We love to be loved in general! But there will usually be one particular expression of love that speaks to us most deeply. One of the biggest causes of dissatisfaction in relationships is giving love in the way we would want to receive it as opposed to in the way our partner wants to receive it. This doesn't fill each other's love tank.

We're going to use little stick-on dots to represent each of the five love languages; this illustrates the principles very clearly, especially if you are a visual learner.

Go get yourself a package of blue, brown, green, yellow, and red dots (often available as yard-sale price-tag stickers at grocery or office-supply stores). It's okay to switch up the colors for what's available.

Words of affirmation—This is the blue dot. Someone who is blue is in need of a little encouragement. This love language typically expresses itself with spoken praise and appreciation. Recognition is important in this language, as is feeling that you have been observed and accurately described.

Acts of service—This is the brown dot. Brown represents wood, which is used to build things; if you are a brown dot, nothing will thrill you more than having someone build or create something for you. You've heard it said that actions speak louder than words. This love language comes with a servant's heart; if you're an "acts of service" kind of person, you feel loved when someone does things that lighten your load.

Receiving gifts—This is the green dot. A green dot says "show me the money!" While gifts can be big or small, for this love language, it's the thought that counts. If this is your love language, you love the idea that someone is thinking of you and puts that thought into action with a gift.

Quality time—This is the yellow dot. Yellow represents the sun coming up. This love language longs for your undivided attention. Whether you are watching TV together or taking an exotic vacation, it is the time spent as a couple that feeds the soul of this lover.

Physical touch—This is the red dot. Red represents passion. Physical touch runs the gamut from hand-holding to sex. With this love language, you just need to reach out and touch your mate.

These descriptions should make it clear which "dot" represents your love language, which speaks most deeply and uniquely to your heart. It is often the one that we ourselves give most freely. Many people who come to the Marriage Boot Camp have an "aha" moment here and realize that they're not using the same love language as their mate. Take your love-dot sticker and put it somewhere you will see it often, such as on the refrigerator or on your vanity mirror, and this will remind you that you have unique needs that you want fulfilled in specific ways.

Similarly, the key to loving your mate is learning to speak his or her love language, and to do that you need to know in exquisite detail the specific way that his or her love language gets fulfilled. Without a complete description, it is almost impossible to get this right.

THE LOVE DOT GAME

Take each of the five love languages and write out a short description of what it would look like to receive love in those ways.

For example, I might say for **Words of Affirmation** that I love when my husband notices when my hair looks great.

For **Acts of Service**, nothing thrills my heart like hearing the vacuum cleaner running and knowing that someone is doing this chore.

In terms of **Receiving Gifts**, I love things for my house.

For **Quality Time**, I love nothing more than sitting and discussing a really interesting book.

For **Physical Touch**, I'm not much of a hugger, but I really love sex with my husband.

Playing the Game with Your Mate

This is a wonderful opportunity to engage your mate. We use the interview technique, where you simply ask your mate to tell you something about themselves and, as we said earlier, everyone loves it when you show interest in them in this way.

You will first tee up the subject and describe the concept of a love language, that each of us has a unique way of wanting to be loved. And you'll go through and describe each of the five love languages. Finally, you will ask your partner to describe what it would look like to them to have each of these love languages fulfilled.

MARRIAGE BOOT CAMP QUICK SCRIPT

To make engaging your mate even easier, here is a quick script as a suggestion of how to get your partner involved:

"I'm reading this book and came across an interesting concept called 'love languages.' It says that each of us feels most loved in one of five different ways. The five love languages are: words of affirmation, acts of service, receiving gifts, quality time, and physical touch. The book had me write down specifically what it would look like to me to get these five languages spoken. What does it look like to you to have these five different love languages spoken?"

Words of Affirmation—Blue Dot
Give an example of what words of affirmation look like to you.

Acts of Service—Brown Dot
Give an example of what acts of service look like to you.

Receiving Gifts—Green Dot
Give an example of what receiving gifts looks like to you.

Quality Time—Yellow Dot
Give an example of what quality time looks like to you.

Physical Touch—Red Dot
Give an example of what physical touch looks like to you.

Discuss each of the love dots and ask your mate which one thrills their heart the most and share the same about your own unique love dot. After this discussion, it should be abundantly clear which "dot" represents each of your love languages, which speaks most deeply and uniquely to each of your hearts. Once you've determined which "dot" represents you and your mate best, stick the colored dot on the front of your shirt to have a visual reminder for the rest of this exercise. (After this exercise, we recommend that you put your love-dot sticker somewhere you will see it often—on the refrigerator or on your vanity mirror—to remind you and your mate that you each have unique needs that must be fulfilled in specific ways.)

We're now going to have you take a deeper dive into your unique love language in an interactive exercise. Take turns and discuss each of the following discussion points.

- Tell your mate what your love language is and give an example of what your love language looks like.
- Tell your mate how you would feel if you had your love language fulfilled on a regular basis.
- Tell your mate what you just learned about him or her.

For Kathy and Gary, this was a groundbreaking exercise. Each of them came to the realization that one of the reasons they were so frustrated with each other is that they were putting in a lot of hard work and not getting the response they wanted. They were *giving* love the way they like to *receive* love. You see, Gary is a green dot. He feels loved when he gets something nice, like a gym membership. Kathy, on the other hand, is a yellow dot, and she wanted Gary to spend time with her, to sit and listen to her as she downloaded all the details of her day.

Gary and Kathy were not only feeling empty, but they were feeling unloved. Gary bought nice things for Kathy and he bought nice things for himself; this was the way he felt loved. He was rewarding his wife the same way he rewards himself. Gary felt frustrated by Kathy when she did not appreciate the things he bought for her and complained about him spending money on himself. Kathy felt rejected and couldn't understand why Gary would want to spend time away from home when she wanted to give him her love in a quality-time kind of way. Now that they understood each other better, we could continue unraveling the conflict they found themselves in.

One last thought. Keep in mind that our mates feed us when they speak our love language. When they neglect or reject our love language, it feels like they are saying "I don't love you." Now that you understand this, you can adjust your "belief" in your ABCs.

THE LOVE BANK

When our mate speaks our love language, it gets directly credited to what we call our "Love Bank." Dr. Willard F. Harley Jr., creator of Marriage Builders and author of the bestseller *His Needs, Her*

Needs: Building an Affair-proof Marriage, says that "inside all of us is a Love Bank with accounts in the names of everyone we know. When these people are associated with our good feelings, 'love units' are deposited into their accounts, and when they are associated with our bad feelings, 'love units' are withdrawn. We are emotionally attracted to people with positive balances and repulsed by those with negative balances. This is the way our emotions encourage us to be with people who seem to treat us well and avoid those who seem to hurt us."

The goal of this section is to demonstrate how feelings of love are *diminished* or *enhanced* by how we invest in each other's "Love Accounts" with deposits and withdrawals.

A "Love Account" is like a checking account. You each make deposits and then write checks against the balance and, like a checking account, you have to stop making withdrawals when your balance gets to zero. However, if you have good credit, you may have overdraft protection and can continue to make withdrawals on the line of credit. If you abuse your overdraft protection and you start writing hot checks, the account gets closed down and you could go to jail!

The same thing happens with your relationship. If you have chronically overdrawn your relationship's Love Account, the result could be disastrous. An overdrawn Love Account often results in nitpicking, criticism, irritability, and a total lack of intimacy. Have you ever spent time with couples who seem to fight about every little thing? When you dig into the specifics of their fights, you often find that there's very little foundation to the fight and it jumps from one little thing to the next little thing. That is usually a symptom of an overdrawn Love Account. With an overdrawn Love Account, the smallest frustration can turn into a bickering match. On the other hand, if you have a full and healthy account, you can weather most of life's frustrations gracefully and it will be very hard to *not* feel the love.

Marcus and Emma's Story

Marcus and Emma came to the Marriage Boot Camp saying that they were both unhappy in their marriage. They'd been together for twenty-six years, having met when they were in junior high. Emma says she thinks Marcus is looking outside their marriage for love and that was the last straw that brought them to us.

Marcus is a very successful attorney, and Emma is a stay-at-home mom whose primary responsibility is to take care of their five children. When we asked them to name one specific thing that they fight about, they even fought about that! They couldn't agree on one thing, so we had to intervene and take a little time to get them to focus on one simple issue. One thing they could agree on is that they fought about Emma's clothing choices.

Marcus claimed that Emma dresses inappropriately—too sexy—and went on to describe a dress she wore to a black-tie function, which had a slit up the leg that was so revealing she could barely sit down. Emma rolled her eyes and said, "I ordered the dress online, and when it came, it was a little bit smaller than I thought, but I didn't have anything else to wear." Marcus said that he felt completely disrespected, but to Emma, Marcus was just giving her a hard time and she was in a lose-

lose situation. She went on to describe a time when she wore a sundress to go to church and Marcus had a fit, saying that it was completely inappropriate. But it was an extremely hot day, and since it was a very nice sundress, she thought it would be just fine. But because of Marcus's disapproval, she changed her clothes and put on a long-sleeved dress. She felt she got the last laugh, though, because when they got to church, the pastor's wife had on a sundress, and she took great pleasure in showing Marcus that he had indeed overreacted.

It appeared to be a fairly simple conflict to resolve; however, just as we got to a point of negotiating Emma's wardrobe in what seemed like a fair compromise, the topic changed. Marcus said Emma focuses too much attention on the way she looks and emphasizes the exterior versus the interior. When we asked Marcus what he felt Emma should be paying more attention to, he said that she needed to develop her interior more. What exactly does she need to develop? we asked. He said she needed to manage their social life better. Emma pointed out that she was the one who arranges their social outings and Marcus just doesn't appreciate how much she does. With taking care of five children and their household, Emma felt overwhelmed by all of her responsibilities.

This session went on and on, from one easily resolved issue to the next, until we finally asked, "What is it that makes you feel the most loved?" Marcus brightened up and said that physical touch (a very clear love language) communicated to him that he is loved and valued and respected. Emma said that the way to her heart was for him to serve her in some way, like taking care of her car (another clear love language, acts of service). Marcus and Emma clearly have very different love languages, and just as clearly, their Love Accounts were empty. Every little irritation became an opportunity to fight. This is often the case with bickerers. The deeper unmet needs get projected onto the little daily imperfections in all of us, looking for a way to get communicated. It's like a game of Whack-a-Mole. Even well-intentioned spouses will take on one little challenge and get it fixed only to have another one pop up. That's because they're not dealing with the underlying conflict.

The challenge was to get Marcus and Emma to understand the fight beneath the fight. We explained to them that many of the little fights would just fall away if they loved each other according to each other's love language and began filling each other's Love Account on a regular basis.

As we continued to dig deeper into the chronic bickering, we finally discovered the root of Marcus's criticism of Emma's wardrobe choices. When Emma dressed in a sexy way (like the sundress), it made Marcus feel the emptiness of his Love Account even more strongly. Marcus said that when she dresses provocatively, his mind goes crazy with wanting to touch her and be touched by her, but she pushes him away. For a man whose love language is physical touch, being pushed away is the same as being told "I don't love you." Emma was having the same problem. She was constantly in service mode to Marcus because this was her way of saying "I love you," while Marcus's response was "whatever." This made Emma feel like he was saying, "I reject your love." They both knew on some level that they loved each other, but neither one of them *felt* loved by the other. I explained to them that it is not enough to *know* that you're loved. You must also *feel* that you are loved.

My next step with Marcus and Emma was to have them dig down deep into what they really needed and wanted from each other and stop mind reading! That clearly hadn't been working.

NEEDS AND WANTS

In addition to having a unique ABC perspective and a unique love language, we all have a complex set of needs and wants that is intertwined with our love language. Many people go through life thinking that *their* love language and *their* needs are universal instead of being unique and personal. Also, many have been taught that it's selfish to ask for your needs to be met and secretly want those things to happen without asking, sometimes growing bitter when they don't. Others feel entitled; they're demanding and will criticize any aspect of the relationship that isn't meeting their needs.

The truth is this: We all have unique needs and we all need our needs to be met. We are one of the few species that is completely dependent on someone meeting our needs when we are born; without that we would die. That dependence continues into adulthood. With that said, we all also need to understand that our needs will be met only imperfectly by imperfect people, and vice versa. The key to this dilemma is understanding and communicating clearly what we need and want from our mates in a way that they can understand.

In order to get your needs met, you first have to be able to communicate what your needs *are*. This may sound simplistic, but in twenty years of counseling, we have found that most couples have not taken the time to sit down and explain what they really want in a specific and actionable way.

Let's take a look at the "Unfulfilled Needs Cycle."

CYCLE OF UNFULFILLED NEEDS

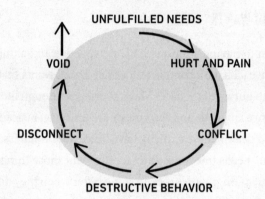

Unfilled needs cause hurt and pain. Hurt and pain cause conflict. Conflict causes destructive behaviors like sarcasm, jabbing, nagging, and shutting down, which causes a separation between spouses. Separation creates a void, an emptiness that seeks to be filled, sometimes in unhealthy ways that lead to further destruction of the relationship.

The way to break the cycle is for you to find a way to fulfill each other's needs, and that begins with communicating your needs in a clear and actionable manner. Now that you know what your love language is and what your mate's love language is, you're both better equipped to inform your partner of your needs and wants so that they can start making deposits and vice versa. We can tell you from experience, if you don't understand the Love Account and how to make deposits, you will be running on empty and every little life irritation will chip away at your marriage.

BOOT CAMP CALL TO ACTION

In this exercise you will be writing down your top four needs and sharing the list with your mate. Here are some examples of the top needs: **respect, affection, honesty, touch, understanding, leadership, security, trust, support, unconditional love, intimacy, communication, equality, appreciation, commitment,** and **fun.**

Remember, each of us defines our needs in a unique and personal way. You will be challenged to be specific about your top needs and then to communicate what this need *looks like* when it is met. This requires you to give clear examples that your mate can understand.

Here's an example of a need—respect. To me respect means that you praise me in public and criticize me in private. It also means that you don't contradict me in front of the children, but take me aside and discuss your difference of opinion privately. Then both of us go to the children together and communicate our position with a united front.

Being able to share your needs and wants in a clear and concise way is the first step toward getting those needs met. Communicating your needs and wants is a win-win for both spouses.

Typically, this discussion can—and will—go south fast, so it is important to avoid the finger-pointing and whining that often accompany a conversation about our needs. This technique will keep you on track.

MARRIAGE BOOT CAMP QUICK SCRIPT

If you need help with an icebreaker, here is a quick script to use:

"The *Marriage Boot Camp* book that I'm reading has a quick exercise to help us communicate our needs and wants without it turning into an argument. I'd love to try this with you so I can hear more about what you need from me. Are you open to this? First, you write down your top four needs or wants. These are the top four things that would make you feel more fulfilled in our marriage. Then you get specific with an example of what it would *look like* to have this need met. Then, after you get your list and your definitions, we can share them. According to the Marriage Boot Camp rules, neither one of us can comment on each other's needs. We simply listen. The book has this list of examples: respect, affection, honesty, touch, understanding, leadership, security, trust, support, unconditional love, intimacy, communication, equality, appreciation, commitment, and fun."

Once you both have your list of needs, here is how you share them:

1. Take turns giving a detailed description of what it would look like to have one of your needs met. Go back and forth until you have shared all four.
2. Exchange lists, so you have your mate's list and vice versa.
3. Look at the list and mirror your mate, that is, express your understanding of each of his or her needs and what it takes to fulfill it.
4. Make a commitment to address the need. Say, "Here's what I'm willing to do to ensure that your need is being met, and I commit to doing this for the next twenty-one days."

DO NOT JUDGE ANYONE'S NEED! Simply say what you are willing to do to fulfill the need.

Now, post the lists in a place, like the refrigerator or the bathroom vanity, where they will be a reminder of your twenty-one-day commitment to each other.

RELATIONSHIP RATING GAME

One thing that we often find missing in relationships is an open and honest dialogue about the quality of the relationship. Our marriages are constantly changing and growing. Let's not wait for boredom to strike or a crisis to hit. Let's get ahead of the criticism before it erupts into conflict. This drill is a good check-in to take the temperature of our relationship and should be done every few months. In this drill, you will rate your relationship, your mate, and yourself on a scale of 1 to 10, with 10 being the best. Don't sugarcoat your scores to look good or to make your mate feel good or to avoid an argument. Dishonesty in your ratings will only rob you of an honest assessment in the end.

Rate Your Relationship from 1 to 10

- Start with a clean sheet of paper.
- Using a marker, cover the entire page with your rating of your relationship on a scale of 1 to 10, with 10 being the highest. Make sure that your number is big enough for your mate to see it, as you will be holding it up to share and discuss.

Show and share your thoughts, going back and forth. Take one minute to tell your mate why you rated your relationship the way you did. This should be a one-way conversation; one will share and one will listen. Simply share your rating; *do not get into a discussion of your rating*.

Rate Yourself as a Mate

You will now rate yourself as a mate on a scale of 1 to 10 based on the following criteria:

- Do you love your mate in spite of their flaws?
- Have you closed down or shut your heart off to your mate?
- Do you make an honest effort to resolve conflicts when they come up?
- Do you make a daily effort to make your mate feel special and loved?
- Do you treat your mate with the same love and respect that you want to receive from them?

Go back and forth and take one minute to tell your mate why you rated yourself the way you did. This should be a one-way conversation; one will share and one will listen.

Rate Your Mate as a Mate

Next you are going to rate your mate as a mate on a scale of 1 to 10. Before you write anything down, ask yourself the following questions:

ELIZABETH AND JIM CARROLL

- Have they loved you unconditionally?
- Are they making an honest effort to meet your needs?
- Are they taking you and/or your relationship for granted?
- Are they doing their fair share as it pertains to daily household chores and helping with the kids?
- Are they understanding and accepting when you make mistakes?

Take one minute apiece to tell your mate why you chose the rating you did. Simply share your rating; *do not discuss your rating.*

Now comes the hard part. You will be discussing your ratings by answering some questions. This would be a perfect opportunity to take stabs at each other. DON'T DO IT! If there is conflict, we ask you to hold your thoughts until you have the chance to read the section on "conflict resolution" in chapter eight. As we are sure you already know, an undisciplined argument will not give you the connection that you long for. Take turns and answer the following questions with your mate:

- **What are you withholding or refusing to do in your relationship and why?** (one minute each to discuss)
- **What's one thing you are willing to do or change to make your relationship better?** (one minute each to discuss)

BRAG ON YOUR MATE—
A SMALL-GROUP EXERCISE

This is an exercise for small groups and a great way to end an evening. The objective of every Marriage Boot Camp drill is to ignite connection between the two of you, and this drill will do that! During this drill, each person stands behind their mate, puts their hands on their shoulders, and gives them a little massage while bragging about their mate to the group. For one minute, they share all of their mate's best qualities. Go around the room until everyone has had an opportunity to share.

This is something you can do in everyday life without anyone else in your social group even knowing that you're practicing a marriage-counseling exercise. Make a point to brag about a recent accomplishment of your mate at least once within his earshot every time you are out socializing. Your mate should make the same effort. The key is to make sure that your mate is in earshot or a part of the conversation so that he or she can hear your accolades.

KEY TAKEAWAYS FOR THIS CHAPTER

- The NUMBER ONE RULE of Marriage Boot Camp: When one person is talking, the other person is listening.
- Understand that every individual views life through a very personal grid.
- Understand your own personal worldview.

- Know yourself well enough to be able to communicate who you are to your partner.
- Know that you are responsible for not only your intentions but also the impact of your behavior. Your intentions can be noble and still have a disastrous impact.
- Learn the skill of mirroring.
- Learn what your love language is and what your mate's love language is.
- Understand the difference between an emotional language and a logical language.
- Articulate your needs and wants.
- Make a commitment to invest in your partner's Love Account.
- Brag on your mate frequently.
- Communication can be hard work, but when you are diligent in learning and practicing how to communicate effectively and lovingly, the rewards will not only be the kind of marriage you always wanted, but more success in your work and better relationships with your children and your friends.

2

....

SEX

....

 Is your sex life all that you dreamed it would be? Do you and your mate communicate openly about sex? Can you describe what you want from sex in clear detail? Do you and your mate fight about sex? Was your first sexual experience wonderful? If you answered negatively to any of these questions, then this chapter is going to provide you with some tools to improve your sex life with your mate. Don't let anyone tell you that sex in a marriage isn't important—it is.

Saul and Erin's Story

Saul and Erin came to the Marriage Boot Camp feeling like they had become no more than roommates. With three small children, financial pressures, and little time for each other, their sex life had dwindled to nothing. They said that all they do is fight or ignore each other, and most of the time they don't even remember what they were fighting about in the first place. They had come to the Marriage Boot Camp to deal with conflict, not their sex life, which they had given up on a long time ago, with Erin shutting down and Saul turning to pornography. But we knew we had to focus our attention on Saul and Erin's sex life, because a marriage will be at risk if it is missing one of its foundational elements: a rich and vibrant sex life.

One of the issues for Saul and Erin was a misunderstanding of the essential differences between men and women. Our bodies are different, and our brains are as different as our bodies. Our chemistry is vastly different: Testosterone fuels a man's aggressive tendencies; estrogen causes women to be natural nurturers.

Saul felt that Erin didn't initiate sex enough, which made him resentful, but underneath the resentment was really a profound sense of rejection. This caused him to check out, avoid the subject, and dabble in pornography. Erin acknowledged Saul's complaint and had made some small attempts to step up her initiative but was never consistent and, frankly, was turned off by her husband's criticism. Erin also felt rejected; she complained, "Am I just not hot enough the way I am? Do I have to act like a porn star to get your attention?"

For the record, women are not natural initiators. Women will step up to be aggressive when the situation calls for it, and men will step up to the plate to be emotionally nurturing when the situation calls for it, but know that it does not necessarily come naturally.

Researchers at the University of Pennsylvania in 2013 found the same thing, as if we needed a brain scan to know this. They analyzed close to one thousand brain scans of men and women and found that the brain circuitry of men and women is very different and points to strengths that heretofore were laughed off as stereotyped bigotry. We're going to get into more detail about the way the different genders' brains work in chapter five, but for now, just accept that men and women are wired differently and have different reactions and responses to the same situations.

No big surprise here. Women are more relational than men, and have highly integrated left/right brains, and men have a more compartmentalized brain with greater abilities in focused tasks. When translated into the bedroom, these differences show up in the University of Pennsylvania survey.

TOP FIVE SEXUAL DESIRES OF MEN

1. More frequent sex
2. To be wanted/adored
3. Visual stimulation
4. Variety and playfulness
5. Oral sex

TOP FIVE SEXUAL DESIRES OF WOMEN

1. Exclusivity
2. Safety
3. Connection
4. Foreplay
5. Romance

As you can see, these desires really don't overlap. So the question is, how do we bridge the gender gap? Let's drill a little deeper and get some more information.

PHASES OF THE SEXUAL EXPERIENCE

There are generally four phases of the sexual experience, and the differences between men and women show up in each.

PHASE	MEN	WOMEN
EXCITEMENT	Visually created	Emotionally created
	Develops fast	Develops slow
	Little focus required	Conscious focus needed
	If lost, easily regained	If lost, more difficult to regain
	Moves quickly to orgasm	Moves more slowly to orgasm
PLATEAU	Generally, very brief	Generally, longer
	Less easily maintained	More easily maintained
	Drive to climax	Slow to climax
ORGASM	Ten to thirteen seconds	Six to sixty seconds
	Limited number of orgasms	Unlimited orgasms
	First orgasm most intense	Later orgasm most intense
RESOLUTION	Rest period needed	No rest period needed
	Sleepy, dreamlike state	Mentally calm but alert

Phase One

So, what we find is that in the EXCITEMENT phase, men are visual, focused, and quick . . . maybe too quick? Men can lose their focus during lovemaking and be able to get right back into sex without hesitation. Women, on the other hand, need to feel emotionally connected and are easily distracted—kids, phones, stupid jokes have no place in the bedroom for women. And once she's distracted? Oy! There's little chance of getting her back in the mood right then and there.

Have you ever listened to women in long-term relationships joking together about what actually goes through their heads during sex? If they're not focused and in the mood, some women make grocery lists, run through their to-do list for when sex is finished, and plan dinner in their heads while their mate is having sex with them. It's totally true. I've heard people joke that if they could only get away with folding laundry in certain positions, they would try. While it's funny, it's also very sad. It shows that their mates don't realize they require a certain level of romance and foreplay to get a woman aroused. Men are like vending machines: Drop in a quarter and get your goodies. Women are like pull-starter lawn mowers: You have to rev her up a bit to get her going.

Phase Two

In the PLATEAU phase, the ability to focus shifts sides. Men want to get to the finish line, while women can hang right here for a while and enjoy the ride. In addition, women become much more open to experimentation once they reach this place. A word to the wise: Wait for the plateau to try that crazy new position!

Phase Three

In the ORGASM phase, the biggest difference is that for men it's one and done, but women are good to go as long as their partners can hang in!

Phase Four

Finally, in the RESOLUTION phase, men are biologically predisposed to rolling over and falling asleep, while women tend to be alert and want to . . . guess what? TALK! While it's portrayed in a comedic fashion all the time, the simple fact is that this difference is completely normal. Couples have to make room for each other's differences without judging each other's needs.

One last point of difference. How long, on average, does it take for a man to reach orgasm versus how long it takes for a woman to reach orgasm?

Average Happy Endings

PHASE	MEN	WOMEN
A	5 Minutes	2 Days
B	10 Minutes	10 Minutes
C	2 Minutes	12 Minutes

The answer is "C."

Guys, what are you going to do with the extra ten minutes? Isn't it interesting that you are given a biological bonus window to consider your woman's need for connection, foreplay, and romance? When you consider that on top of everything else, we have a math problem, it is a miracle that we *ever* get it right!

Here's another difference to consider. Men are interested in their woman's lady parts, and women are interested in men's hearts. In other words, most women won't give you the green light to "pet the kitty" until you first touch her heart, because she needs to feel connected before having sex. Men are the opposite; sex is often the way that they feel connected, and only after that will they give a woman access to their heart.

You might be wondering, "Why would we be designed this way?" Here's your answer: because it creates the perfect standoff. The key to getting what you want is giving your mate what he or she wants. It is a brilliant strategy to keep two people connected and helps avoid the poison of selfishness that can destroy any relationship.

For Saul and Erin, a little education went a long way. Understanding that a man and a woman are wired differently helped them revise some of the assumptions they held. Instead of seeing the other's behavior as evidence of rejection and lack of attraction, they were able to understand that they were simply navigating sex in a very typical way for their gender.

IMPRINTING

There were, however, some additional speed bumps on the road to sexual satisfaction. Both Saul and Erin had early sexual experiences that continued to affect their present situation.

A babysitter seduced Saul when he was twelve years old. He never saw this as a problem; in fact, he talked about it with a bit of pride and bravado. What guy wouldn't brag about being taken by a hot teenage girl? But when we dug a little deeper, he admitted that he had been frightened and embarrassed by the situation and had never discussed it with his wife until Marriage Boot Camp. He hadn't seen how this early sexual experience had played out in his life, driving him into relationships with several highly aggressive, desperate females.

Erin, on the other hand, came from a close-knit Christian family and had saved herself for marriage. When Saul met Erin, he described her as being "a breath of fresh air," independent, deeply moral in her Christian faith, and devoted to her family. These were some of the traits that made him decide that she was "the one."

While Erin took the sexual moral high ground, needling Saul about his "checkered past" and his "addiction" to pornography, upon investigation we came to discover that Erin used her religion as a wall to keep from feeling vulnerable. She had also had a damaging sexual experience early in life. A youth pastor she'd admired had touched Erin inappropriately, and she'd come away feeling that no man could be trusted sexually.

These first sexual experiences had a profound effect on Saul and Erin. We call this imprinting. The first experience of sex is so powerful, both psychologically and chemically, that it gets "imprinted" in our minds, and we then go about trying to re-create this experience for the rest of our lives.

If the first sexual experience is with someone you barely know, imagine how this gets revisited in marriage: non-relational, impersonal recreational sex. This is the case for many men. Women are more likely to be invested in the relationship with their first partner, so if he never calls and treats the experience as impersonal, she begins to think of sex as unimportant, perhaps something to avoid—because this is her imprint. Imagine how that gets played out over and over. Saul and Erin had some work to do unraveling some of their early sexual imprinting and getting to a place of viewing sex properly, as a beautiful, bonding, necessary aspect of their marriage.

PORNOGRAPHY

We would be remiss not to talk about the kind of imprinting that comes from pornography because that can also be a factor in sexual problems. If a man spends a great deal of time gratifying himself with, for example, pornography that features large-breasted women, he will bring this imprint into the marital bedroom and may be unsatisfied with his partner's physique.

Understand that the appeal of pornography has a lot to do with feeling accepted. It never rejects you. It always welcomes you, wants you, and says yes. Unfortunately, this is false intimacy, and it can hinder true intimacy in that it compromises your ability to bond with a real person in a healthy way. Here's the kicker: False intimacy leaves you a little bit emptier than when you started, and this deficit then needs to be filled at a higher and higher dose, almost like a drug addiction. That's why pornography can be considered addictive. True intimacy, on the other hand, leaves you feeling loved and full to overflowing. It multiplies rather than subtracts.

Saul and Erin were in a common cycle that often ends in the stalemate of a sexual cold war.

- It starts with a misunderstanding of the normal biological differences between men and women, causing negative judgments to be passed—men are animals, women are cold fish, etc.
- The misunderstanding gets interpreted as judgment and rejection, which compromises the bond between spouses.
- The response to the perceived rejection creates secondary problems such as asexuality, criticism, coldness, pornography.
- Conflict ensues over the secondary problem and the blame game starts, which results in the unsolved circularity of a stalemate.

THE INITIATION-RESPONSE DILEMMA

Almost every sexual relationship hits a speed bump over who initiates sex and how often. There is almost always one partner with a higher sex drive than the other—usually the man—and this person ends up initiating sex most of the time. As we saw, Saul wanted Erin to initiate more, and Erin didn't step up to the plate because it wasn't in her nature and she had the lower sex drive. This is a recipe for conflict and hurt.

Rather than trying to make things "fair" by asking Erin to initiate sex more often, Marriage Boot Camp prefers to get underneath this potential power struggle and strive for a solution that works for both parties. One of the tools that we use is sex scheduling. Believe it or not, this one simple tool will not only give you a great sex life, but it can also solve a conflict that couples often don't realize is related to sex: power struggles.

Nathan and Jordana's Story

Nathan complained that he always felt sexually neglected, and his wife, Jordana, said she felt constantly sexually harassed. She confessed that she sometimes made Nathan beg for sex while she played hard to get. She enjoyed the cat-and-mouse game and the sense of power that it gave her. What she didn't realize was the cost. This game made Nathan feel anxious and rejected. He responded to this sense of rejection by becoming more aggressive. The more aggressive Nathan became, the more Jordana pushed back. This frustration started to bleed into other areas of their marriage and the power struggle cropped up over little things, like where to have dinner.

In order to remove the power struggle from the frequency-of-sex issue, we sat them down and had them negotiate a literal calendar for sex. Each partner simply had to answer the question "How often do you want have sex?" Jordana wanted sex four times a week and Nathan wanted sex every day, sometimes twice a day. So they compromised and agreed on a schedule of six times a week and even put alerts on their phones. As Nathan and Jordana humorously told us later, now Nathan will look at his watch as the minutes count down and, when the alert goes off, he yells, "Bingo!"

So that's it. Schedule sex, and gone will be the power struggle and the anxiety over whether or not you're going to get laid. Another added benefit is that the schedule gives you time to prepare your heart, mind, or body as needed. Intentionality is the key.

The point of sex scheduling is simply to take the stress out of the initiation-response dilemma, but first you have to ask yourself a few questions:

- Do you believe that sex is important to your marriage?
- Are you willing to give of yourself sexually to your mate?
- Are you tired of the awkward, stressful, and sometimes conflicted relationship in the bedroom?

One of the underlying principles that make marriage work is a giving attitude and a desire to please your mate. And one of our Marriage Boot Camp principles is this: Make every effort to never say no to your mate!

Okay, we know what you're thinking: give up your right to say no? As if! But trust us; this technique works to make *both* of you happier. In a great marriage, you come to realize that your body is now not just your own but your mate's as well, and vice versa; your mate's body belongs to you, too. Two become one. Somehow it's easier to view "what's mine is yours and yours is mine" in the context of material possessions, but we have found that it also applies to healthy sexuality. In marriage, we make a leap of connection that includes finances, children, and even our bodies. Sometimes you will have to say no, but strive to be as giving and generous with your mate as you can.

A Final Word on Chemistry

Oxytocin is the hormone that causes us to bond with a partner. It's what made you fall in love in the first place, and it's still available anytime to help you diminish negative imprinting and rebond with your spouse. Here are some ways to create positive imprinting:

- Make love with your eyes open, with the lights on, so that you will visually bond during your sexual experience.
- Make love regularly to reinforce the reprogramming.
- Connect with your mate by talking to each other during sex in a nurturing, loving, or playful way. Let your voices get imprinted in each other's minds.

If you are willing to be educated and intentional, sex can be absolutely amazing despite early mistakes and our innate differences. This is particularly important if you've been the victim of abuse. Erasing the imprint of another's cruelty can be difficult, but it is not impossible. It takes time, patience, and dedication. If you use the steps above religiously, you will find that practice makes perfect. And what is more fun to practice than sex?

BOOT CAMP CALL TO ACTION I—GETTING TO KNOW YOU

The first step to creating a vibrant and satisfying sex life is understanding yourself sexually. Set aside some time to write down your answers to the following questions:

- What was you earliest sexual experience?
- How do your early experiences affect you today?
- What do you want most in your sex life?
- What stops you from having the kind of sex life that you want?
- What you are willing to do to create the kind of sex life that you want?

Engaging Your Mate

This is a wonderful opportunity to engage your mate in a discussion about sex. We use the interview technique again. You're simply asking your mate to tell you something about himself and, let's face it, everyone loves it when you show interest in them in this way—even when you've been together a very long time.

MARRIAGE BOOT CAMP QUICK SCRIPT

Since not all of us have a natural ability to open up communication about sex, we use the Marriage Boot Camp Quick Script to give you a how-to model for getting this conversation started:

"I've just finished reading a chapter in *Marriage Boot Camp* on sex and would love to share some of this with you. I learned a lot, and because I love you, I want us to have the best possible sex life that we can have. They claim that there are dramatic differences in how men and women approach sex, not so much because our bodies are different but because our brains are different. I'd like to share some of this material with you because I found it fascinating and I learned a lot." [Read back through the material together.] "They list five questions that can help a couple improve their sex life, and I've taken some time to write down my answers. I'd love to hear how you answer these questions and want to share what I wrote. Are you open to that?"

If your mate is willing to engage with you, have him write down his answers to the five Marriage Boot Camp questions. This will definitely get the conversation started.

BOOT CAMP CALL TO ACTION II—SEX SCHEDULE

As we saw with Jordana and Nathan, this simple and practical tool solved many of their marital problems—sex initiation, power struggles, feeling rejected. All of these issues improved for them, and it can work for you too!

Get into a dyad with your mate; that is, sit facing each other, knees to knees, making eye contact. Share your answer to this question: Ideally, how often per week would you like to have sex? If your answers are different, negotiate a compromise. Sounds simple, but don't be deceived. Talking about your needs, particularly your sexual needs, goes deep into vulnerable places.

MARRIAGE BOOT CAMP QUICK SCRIPT

Since this can be a challenging conversation, here is a Marriage Boot Camp Quick Script to give you a model for getting this topic started:

"I've just finished reading about Jordana and Nathan in the *Marriage Boot Camp* chapter on sex and would love to share some of it with you. One of the tools they use is 'sex scheduling.' Ideally, how often would you like to have sex per week?"

At this point you can share your answer to this question and the two of you can negotiate a compromise if needed. Try to get as detailed as possible: not just number of times per week but which days of the week, daytime or nighttime, type of sex (intercourse, oral, cuddling, etc.). Then you can do what Jordana and Nathan did: Put alerts on your phone so that you never forget!

Some of you might be worried that this approach takes all the spontaneity and surprise out of your sex life. Not at all. This exercise will free you up to be really creative: lingerie, music, wine, costumes, role-playing . . . The possibilities are endless!

Great Sex in Five Minutes

When your scheduled "appointment" arrives, follow these five simple steps to great intimate sex—sex that renews, refreshes, and refuels your relationship. The secret is the first five minutes. Follow this simple Marriage Boot Camp drill and after that, anything goes.

Step 1—RELEASE: Make eye contact and make a commitment to release all bitterness and resentment for the moment. Remember that your thoughts determine your feelings and you can choose your thoughts. Choose wisely. Say, "I choose to hold nothing against you right now," and mean it! Do not focus your mind on bitterness; this will turn your thoughts in the wrong direction for a successful romantic sexual interlude.

Step 2—LOVE SHOWER: Take your spouse's hand, make eye contact, and express all the things you love about him or her, including the things you loved when you first met. Women should probably go first, as they are often better at articulating their feelings.

Step 3—FACE-TO-FACE: Stand face-to-face, rubbing cheek to cheek or nose to nose. Close your eyes. Just let your mind relax. Focus on this moment only! Forget about any of the stressors in your life.

Step 4—BODY-TO-BODY: Hold your mate. Wrap your arms around your loved one. Lean in and just enjoy each other's warmth. Allow your body to relax for one minute.

Step 5—MOUTH-TO-MOUTH: Take one minute and just kiss your mate. Nice, slow kisses. Set the mood for the rest of the time.

The foundation is now set. The truth is, most women need a bridge from their normal life to their sexual life, while most men can just jump the fence. But even fence jumpers will find sex more deeply satisfying when they know that their partner is feeling sexually connected. Practice these five one-minute steps and you can have intimate sex that reboots your relationship every time.

3

MONEY

 **QUICK QUIZ** Do you fight about money? Do you seem to have the same argument over and over? Do you have stress in your relationship because of financial irresponsibility? Does your financial situation make you feel frightened of the future? Are you and your mate completely honest about all of your financial dealings? If you answered negatively to any of these questions, then you will benefit greatly from this chapter.

Elizabeth's Story

When Jim and I got married, I transitioned from life as a single working mother raising two children, putting one through college, and driving a ten-year-old car, to having a husband who would prove to be a very generous provider. One of the first things Jim did was surprise me with a new car. That really pissed me off. I was doing just fine, thank you very much, and I did not need a sugar daddy. I figured that, since we were combining incomes, I could buy myself a new car with no problem, in my own time, in my own way. *Humph.* Clearly, the meaning of this new car purchase, or the "B" in our "Action-Belief-Consequence," was very different for each of us. Jim expresses his love with gifts because that's how he enjoys receiving it. But I perceived the gesture as a statement that I hadn't been able to take care of myself adequately before we were married. And the fight was on . . .

Todd and Courtney's Story

Todd and Courtney came to the Marriage Boot Camp worn out from a chronic fight. They had a blended family, each of them bringing two adult children to the new marriage. Their chronic battle was over how much money to give to the four children. Todd was financially successful and had always been very generous with his children. Excessively so, in his new wife's opinion. Courtney had been a struggling single mom before she met Todd, and she had always been very frugal with her children. Todd wanted to maintain his current level of generosity to his children, but Courtney thought they should give less to his children and more to hers, so it was a level playing field. If not, she suggested Todd simply reduce the amount of money he gave his children to match the amount given to her children. Todd felt that giving anything less to his children was unfair.

They came into the Marriage Boot Camp to get help with this financial impasse, but the true source of their conflict was a much larger issue lurking below the surface. Before we move on, let's take a look at conflict over money.

In 2012 in *U.S. News & World Report*, Daniel Bortz cites the American Institute of Certified Public Accountants' survey of married or cohabitating couples that found that disagreements over finances were more likely to turn into a full-blown argument than issues surrounding children, chores, work, or friends.

And the data only gets worse, Bortz reports. A 2011 study by Jeffrey Dew at Utah State University found that the divorce rate doubles for married couples who fought about money once a week, as compared with those who fought about money less than once a month.

Mitch Temple, writing for the website Focus on the Family, says that money is one of the major causes of friction in marriage and is reflected in the rise in popularity of prenuptial agreements and separate bank accounts. Underlying this friction is often a lack of trust and a preference for self-sufficiency above interdependence with your spouse. This is a real change from the way the world worked twenty or thirty years ago.

THE ISSUE BELOW THE ISSUE—THE CORE ISSUE

Why is money the issue that couples fight about most? Because money is symbolic of so many other things! We may resolve a haggle over a certain expense, but the problem is that the issue below the issue still remains.

"Money doesn't just represent money; it represents love, power, control, self-esteem, freedom," says Olivia Mellan, money coach and author of *Money Harmony: Resolving Money Conflicts in Your Life and Relationships*. We would also add "family culture" and "financial personality" to the list of factors that create financial conflict in any relationship.

Whenever you find yourself having the same fight over and over, it indicates that the real problem may be the "issue below the issue" or the "core issue." If core issues are not dealt with, surface issues—like finances—will continue to rear their ugly heads.

So let's look at the most common issues below the issue of money:

Love—If your love language is gifts, the representation of money as love is obvious. You feel most loved when someone spends money on you, and you feel unloved when you are not being showered with gifts. Again, there's nothing wrong with this, although gold diggers and sugar babies have given the "love as money" formula a truly bad name. So let's make a distinction here, for the record. Feeling loved when someone buys you something is very different from flattering somebody in order to get money or have them buy you material things. If you are fighting about money because you don't feel loved, therein lies the core issue.

Power—Having a lot of money gives you a lot of power. As with love, this is not necessarily a bad thing. Many wealthy people use their money for philanthropic ends, to better the lives of those less fortunate. On the other hand, if your spouse uses having money to lord it over you and get you to do what he or she wants, then you're in a power struggle.

Control—Let's state the obvious: Having money gives you a certain level of control over your life. Money can make life easier, and give you choices and options in many areas. But life can never be completely controlled. If you are striving after money because you think it will make life predictable, easy, and trouble-free, you are sadly mistaken. If you are fighting with your mate about money when the truth is that you actually want more control over your lives and want them to be more predictable, then you have just identified the core issue.

Self-esteem—Being financially secure is a great way to boost your self-esteem. It can make you feel good about yourself to have achieved success; you're validated as a responsible, hard-working soul and a wise investor. If, however, you need money to boost your low self-esteem because you think that it is impressive to have a lot of money, then you are locating your worth outside yourself, in your W-2 and in the approval or envy of others. If you are fighting with your mate about money, ask yourself if self-esteem is actually the core issue.

Freedom—Money definitely gives us freedom. The more money we have, the more freedom we have: the freedom to try new business ventures, to leave a job that is no longer satisfying, or even to retire. Money gives us the freedom to buy things like a house, a car, an expensive vacation, or a great education for our children. But money does not give us complete freedom, especially in marriage. Relationships always require that we consider the needs of others as well as our own. If you are fighting about how you will spend your money, you may actually be fighting about the *constraints* that a relationship puts on how you spend your money. Do you feel like you don't want to have to answer to anybody about how you spend? Then you have just identified the core issue.

Family Culture—How we grew up has a tremendous effect on how we view and deal with money. If you grew up in a financially responsible family, then it's likely that you will be a financially responsible adult. If, however, you grew up in a financially irresponsible family or an impoverished household, you may have some bad habits to break, such as not understanding how to handle money or being extremely cautious and rigid when it comes to spending. In conflicts about money, it is very important to ask the question "Is this familiar?" If you are reenacting some of the challenges that you saw in your family growing up, then it's likely that you need to work with your mate on creating a new, collaborative culture regarding money.

Financial Personality—We have to accept that fundamentally some people are spenders and some people are savers. Spenders often want a great deal of freedom, and savers often want a great deal of control. It's not unusual to find a saver married to a spender. The "opposites attract" notion, in its healthiest expression, is about complementarity and balance. We are attracted to those who "complete us." A frank conversation about the type of personality that you have would likely yield beneficial results. From there the negotiations begin. Compromising and appreciating the complementary role that your mate plays in your life is part of the solution.

CREATING A BUDGET

As we have seen, conflict in marriage about money has many different facets. Now that you understand the concept of the "issue below the issue" and you have your core issue in your sights, many of you are still left with the challenge of managing money as a couple. The first thing you will have to do is establish a budget. It is important to establish a budget because a lot of conflict has to do with assumptions and emotions. Establishing a budget will take all the guesswork out of your financial disagreements, and a lot of the emotional heat as well. Your budget is black-and-white, just facts and numbers. Jim and I use a simple Excel spreadsheet, but there are many different ways this can be done.

There is a lot of information available on how to create and maintain a budget, but Miriam Caldwell, an expert on finances for people in their twenties, breaks it out into three simple steps in her article on Moneyfor20s.about.com about "How to Budget as a Couple."

1. First you need to determine the cost of your essential household needs. This would include things such as rent or mortgage payments, property taxes, tuition, utilities, commuting costs, groceries, car payments, health insurance, and debt payments. (We also recommend including a fixed amount to put into your savings account

every month.) These are your fixed costs that need to be met before you begin to budget for your discretionary purchases. Some fixed costs are almost impossible to change (such as student loan payments), while with others there is wiggle room. For example, you could save money by buying a less expensive car, cutting back on groceries, or renting a smaller place.

2. Once you've determined your household needs, you can begin to talk about individual desires. These can include everything from gym memberships, clothing, and haircuts to eating out, movie tickets, or buying Christmas gifts. Some couples find easy agreement on what constitutes a reasonable amount to spend on these discretionary purchases, but sometimes it's a real struggle. For example, men and women often expect to spend very different amounts on things like clothes and hair care, and one of you may have an expensive hobby that the other doesn't share. You may be inclined to give your spouse a hard time about how much he spends on video games, or how much she spends on spin classes. Recognize that your needs and wants are different, and that's okay. It's important to compromise. Look at your income and decide together how much you can afford on joint expenses such as dining out. For separate purchases, rather than fight about whether it's reasonable to spend twenty dollars on a manicure, you may want to set up an allowance for each of you to spend on your wants without being accountable to the other person.

3. Once you have set up your budget, you both need to take

part in tracking your spending. A weekly meeting usually works well. During this meeting you can discuss where you are in working toward your goals. Additionally, you can talk about how much money you have left in each category versus any planned expenses. You can adjust your categories as needed. At the beginning, you may need to go over this every night, but eventually you can do it just once a week. Financial software can be helpful (we like ones that you can sync on your phones), but work out whatever system you prefer.

Another tried-and-true program that we highly recommend is Dave Ramsey's class, Financial Peace University, and his book *The Total Money Makeover*. Dave Ramsey gives you not only a money-management philosophy, but worksheets and budgeting ideas that will work for anyone.

Dave encourages you to "Break the cycle, change your family tree, live on less than you make, save for a rainy day, and live like no one else." He recommends that you start with a budget that he calls the "Zero-Based Budget," where you allocate every penny of your income to a category. Then you set up the "envelope system" for all of the non-debt categories. You use one envelope for each category and put cash in each envelope according to your budgeted amount. Studies have shown that saving is easier because it is psychologically much harder to spend cash than it is to use a credit or debit card. Then you start taking baby steps, one at a time, so that financial planning won't overwhelm you and you can move toward financial freedom.

Here is a synopsis of Dave Ramsey's Seven Baby Steps:

Baby step one is to break your current financial cycle by creating a small emergency fund. He recommends that you put a thousand dollars into a "rainy day fund" so that, when life happens, you will at least be somewhat prepared. He says to get creative, babysit, have a garage sale, but nail the first step ASAP!

Baby step two is to get rid of debt. This is a process in which you attack and eliminate each of your debts (except your house payment), from smallest to largest.

Baby step three is to create a substantial emergency fund that amounts to three to six months of living expenses in cash to cover unexpected expenses. This is a separate and sacred, never-touch-it account for emergencies only.

Baby step four is to start long-term investing—saving for retirement. He recommends that you save fifteen percent of your income and invest this money into growth stock mutual funds with long track records.

Baby step five is saving for college. He recommends avoiding student loans at all cost; choose only schools that you can afford. If worse comes to worst, make your kids work and put themselves through college.

Baby step six is to pay off your mortgage. Many financial planners disagree with this, but Ramsey advises, and we agree, that you should take all of the money you have after the first six steps and throw it at your house. He says that most people who follow his program are able to pay off their house in six or seven years.

Baby step seven is to build wealth and give. It follows that if you are managing your assets wisely you will start to build wealth, and with the financial freedom you've now obtained, you are able to give to others in need and causes that you believe in. As you will read in chapter nine, there comes a season of life called "generativity," when having a sense of purpose and giving back becomes the core driver of fulfillment, and without this a person is left feeling disconnected and useless. You cannot be successful in this stage of life if you are financially imprisoned.

The objective of these steps is to create the life and the marriage that *you* envision for yourselves, a life that is unique to the two of you and a blessing to your families.

For the Newlyweds

We hope this doesn't apply to you, but some people get married without knowing exactly how much money—or how much debt—their new mate is bringing into the marriage. All of the principles set forth in this chapter apply especially to the crazy-in-love crowd! If that describes you, it's imperative that the two of you do every exercise in this chapter. Make sure that you discuss your unique financial personalities, your family culture, your expectations and ambitions. While most couples have discussed these things before marriage, they haven't always gotten specific enough. Perhaps one of them has a *lot* of family money and is leery of gold diggers, or her partner doesn't want to be seen as greedy if he opens the discussion. Debt is also a taboo subject for a lot of people. Let's face it, telling someone you hope will commit to you that you have two maxed-out credit cards or loads of student debt can be scary. The thing is, when you get married, you become one; what's mine is yours and vice versa. If you cannot be honest and truthful with each other, your marriage is built on a very shaky foundation.

Melanie and Matt's Story

Melanie and Matt had been friends for years when they discovered their mutual romantic attraction. Both of them were single at the time, and it wasn't long before Matt moved into Melanie's condo. They were engaged six months later and married six months after that. Melanie had a solid job with the state and knew that Matt's job in hospitality didn't provide the same benefits, so they planned to put him on her insurance. This conversation would've been a great entrée into the discussion that they *didn't* have. She also knew that his income fluctuated based on the time of year, and she assumed that once they were married, they'd make a budget together and save for the leaner times.

Unfortunately, Matt had not been forthright with Melanie about the way his pay actually worked and how much money he actually earned. He never let her see a pay stub, and they didn't merge any accounts. He continued to contribute the same amount to the household monthly bills that he had when they were first living together, not taking into account that she was paying his health insurance out of her paycheck every month. And there were lots of other shared expenses that went onto Melanie's personal credit card because Matt didn't have any credit cards, something that should have been another red flag to her about a man in his midthirties.

One day, a letter arrived for Matt that Melanie opened before he got home from work because the return address scared her. She learned that Matt had almost fifty thousand dollars in student debt and that not only had he not been making payments, but he apparently had been trying to hide from his debtors and they had just tracked him down to her condo.

When Matt got home from work, Melanie confronted him about the letter and he exploded. It took weeks for them to de-escalate and have a serious discussion about how damaging this was to their marriage. They eventually decided to seek help.

At the Marriage Boot Camp, Matt and Melanie finally came to grips with the "issue below the issue." Matt had grown up in poverty but hadn't let it hold him back and had done pretty well for himself. He was a big dreamer, a "free spirit" where money was concerned. But that didn't mean he wasn't concerned about the debt he was piling up. In fact, he was embarrassed, so he worked harder and harder to keep the problem hidden. Melanie was responsible with money, always attentive to the nuts and bolts of insurance, taxes, and the 401(k)s of life. Little did they realize at the time, but they needed each other. Matt brought a lighthearted, fun spirit to Melanie's life, and Melanie brought responsibility to his, things they both craved. Once they realized this core difference and came to appreciate the way they complemented each other, the conflict de-escalated and they were ready to face the problem together. Well, *problems*: Not only did they have a money problem, but they also had an honesty problem. Matt came completely clean, sharing his fears and his shame and vowing to never keep anything from Melanie again. After a lot of hard work, Melanie forgave him, and they locked arms to fight the dragon. Melanie dragged a financial adviser and an accountant into the process—family members, since they really couldn't afford to hire out—and Matt part-nered with her to face their financial situation head-on as a team, starting with a budget. It was not untenable—it could be fixed. Matt and Melanie finally agreed to adjust their life plans so that they could get his debt paid off before anything else; they'd hold off on starting a family until they could better afford a baby. At last they were working together as teammates instead of adversaries.

Lessons learned. When you decide to get married, it's time to lay all the cards and accounts on the table—the good, the bad, and the ugly. If there's something you're hiding from, be honest and open and tackle it together. If you lie, if you hide your pre-vious financial mistakes, they will come back to bite you, and your spouse will be bitten, too.

Do not be judgmental if you learn that your mate's financial status is less than optimal—be understanding and simply ac-cept it for what it is. It's best to discuss these things before you exchange vows, but it's never too late. Being married means you have to have a team approach to solving your problems. Say things like "I know this terrifies you, but it doesn't make me love you any less; let's figure out the best way to make this work for both of us. I don't want you to have to keep worrying about this alone." You will be amazed by the response you get to such a generous acceptance of your mate's earlier mistakes.

The Rest of Elizabeth's Story

Well, Jim and I had some work to do around our core issues at the beginning of our marriage. Or rather, I had some work to do around my core issues. I had always been financially independent and worked very hard to be that way. I grew up not knowing if I would have shoes for school or sometimes if there would be enough to eat. I never trusted anyone to take care of me—I would do that for myself. And I made sure that my children were well cared for because I never wanted them to experience the insecurity that I once felt. I still feel that knot of insecurity in my stomach whenever I go shopping, even to the grocery store, and I find myself having to use soothing self-talk just to get through Costco.

Jim did not grow up the way I grew up, and as an adult, he has always been a hard worker and a successful businessman. He's extremely generous and was devastated by my reaction to the new car. He was trying to show me love, but I felt like he was trying to put me down and diminish the value I brought to the relationship. Worse yet, I felt that he was questioning my integrity by putting me in the same category as some of the materialistic women he had dated in the past. I did not understand all of this when we got into the first fight, but now Jim and I know that this is a "hot button" issue for me. P.S. After we worked through it, Jim sent flowers to my office with a card saying, "I'm sorry I bought you a car." After that, the joke around the office whenever Jim sent me flowers was, "What did he buy you now?"

BOOT CAMP CALL TO ACTION

Think about your own personal financial personality and write down your answers to the following questions:

WHICH BEST DESCRIBES THE ROLE MONEY PLAYS IN YOUR LIFE?

- Security: Money helps you feel safe and secure.
- Status: Money helps you create a positive image.
- Selfless: Money helps you feel good by giving to others.
- Free Spirit: Money is not a priority for your carefree lifestyle.
- Goal-oriented: Money helps you achieve your goals.
- Spontaneous: Money encourages you to enjoy the moment.

   (From Syble Solomon, the creator of Money Habitudes, a program that helps people talk about money and understand their financial personalities.)

ARE YOU A SPENDER OR A SAVER? CONSIDER THESE QUESTIONS:

- How did your family handle finances and how does this affect you today?
- What are your concerns or desires regarding your financial situation?
- What do you need from your mate regarding your financial situation?
- How transparent are you and your mate with each other?

Engaging Your Mate

This is a wonderful opportunity to engage your mate in a discussion about money. We use the interview technique, as before, only this time we're talking about money. You're simply asking your mate to tell you something about himself that will open up the entire topic for discussion.

MARRIAGE BOOT CAMP QUICK SCRIPT

Since not all of us have a natural ability to open up communication with our mates, here's a how-to model to get this conversation started. Give it a try:

"I've just finished reading a chapter in *Marriage Boot Camp* on money and would love to share some of this with you. I learned a lot, and because I love you, I want us to have complete peace and security about our financial situation. They claim that when we fight about money, the issue is rarely actually about money; it usually represents deeper issues. They ask a series of questions so that you can get a better handle on how each of us relates to money. I've taken some time to write down my answers. I'd love to share what I wrote and hear how you answer these questions. Are you open to that?"

If your mate is willing to engage with you, use the Marriage Boot Camp questions and write down your mate's answers. This will definitely get the conversation started on a topic that may normally be taboo around your household. Finally, commit to creating and maintaining a realistic budget. This will take the emotion out of the topic of money and keep you both accountable and transparent. Go back to the section of this chapter that gives you an overview of budgeting as well as recommendations for programs and software that can be used to accomplish your financial goals.

KEY TAKEAWAYS FOR THIS CHAPTER

- Money is one of the top causes of conflict in marriage.
- Money is often just the tip of the iceberg, with the real issue below.
- Our relationship to money reveals much about our personality.
- We must have complete transparency regarding our relationship to money.
- Creating and maintaining a budget is one of the best ways to avoid conflicts about money.

4

CHORES

 QUICK QUIZ Is he a neat freak and you're not? Do you and your mate fight about whose job it is to do which task? Do you feel overwhelmed by your responsibilities while your mate wonders what you do all day? Can you describe how you think the chores should be divided in clear detail? If you can relate to these questions, pay close attention. This chapter will give you some tools that make sharing responsibilities a lot easier.

Do you feel like we're changing gears on you quickly here? Well, we're not. Money and chores are very similar in that they both can be "presenting issues" rather than "core issues" when couples are fighting. Whether bickering about credit-card debt or who last did the dishes, the truth is that couples are usually fighting about something else. In chapter three we talked about identifying the issue below the issue. In this chapter we will be doing the same.

Are you surprised that doing chores is one of the top-ten issues that couples fight about? You see, if a couple can't work together to make their household run smoothly, it affects every other aspect of their relationship. A woman with a to-do list ten miles long isn't going to be focusing much on her husband. Likewise, the husband who just got yelled at for not doing the things on his "honey do" list probably isn't interested in giving his mate the time and attention she needs in order to have a fulfilling marriage.

As we said with conflicts about money, chores may not actually be the *real* issue, but a concrete representation of some deeper issues the couple is struggling with. When you're able to create a reasonable and specific list of household responsibilities and chores and split them equitably, peace can reign in the land. When one half of a couple feels put-upon, overwhelmed, and unappreciated, this is more than just an issue of time and task management. It is an issue of the heart.

Let's first take a look at some interesting research. According to Pew Research, chores ranked in the top three factors of what constituted a successful or unsuccessful marriage. The CLR Chore Wars Report looked at how opposite sexes clean. Not surprisingly, sharing household duties meant different things to men and women: "In fact, sixty-nine percent of women felt they did most of the work around the house, while fifty-three percent of the men disagreed, feeling they worked just as hard as the women when it came to cleaning up. The survey also found that arguing over chores was extremely common; about one out of five Americans admitted to arguing about housework on a monthly basis," says Dr. Robi Ludwig, a relationships expert who participated in the Chore Wars study. And while most women work outside the home, they're still doing most of the household chores, according to Sheri Stritof, a marital advice expert for About.com. This may sound harmless; however, "Those who felt overburdened by household chores and felt like they did most, if not all, of the housework showed a greater level of built-up resentment toward their partners over time. And the couples who felt chores were more equally shared felt happier toward their partners and happier about their marriages in general," Ludwig says.

Part of the problem is that there simply have not been clear models of what a dual-income, well-managed household looks like. Most married couples today grew up in a family in which their mothers did more housework than their fathers. Typically, mothers took care of the children and the house and did all the shopping, cooking, and cleaning, while dads mostly did "handyman chores," such as unclogging drains, mowing the lawn, changing the oil, and cleaning out the gutters—and only on weekends! Whether or not that's how you grew up, it certainly isn't how things work in the world today and why it may not be working for you as a couple. Stereotypical household responsibilities have to be set aside. It makes no sense to expect the wife to be on a first-name basis with the dry cleaner if the shop is on the husband's way to work. And if he's better in the kitchen than she is, why shouldn't he be the primary chef in the house?

Now, you might assume the solution to arguments about chores is to simply balance out the labor. In fact, though, at Marriage Boot Camp we have found that splitting the chores fifty-fifty is not always the answer! An unequal division of labor can still result in a solid and cohesive marriage, while perfect balance may not lead to happiness. Like money, there are many, many layers to this one issue, and taking a superficial division-of-labor perspective may not give you the answer. The real question is, How do you feel about your mate and about yourself in relation to the issue of chores?

John and Tabitha's Story

When we asked John and Tabitha what they wanted to get out of their Marriage Boot Camp experience, they said they wanted to grow in the areas of communication and respect—but the problem they complained about the most was *chores*! Tabitha felt she was constantly picking up, cleaning, and preparing for the next activity, meal, or obligation and resented it when John would come home and complain about a mess. He accused Tabitha of setting booby traps throughout the house to jump out at him whenever he opened a cabinet or door. Tabitha responded that she tries all day to be as productive as possible and that John could certainly organize a drawer or a closet instead of blaming her for its disorder.

We could see from their interchanges that John was putting Tabitha into defense mode and that the feeling of "not meeting John's expectations" was hurtful to her. The pressure of keeping the entire house clean and keeping all cabinets, drawers, and closets in perfect order all of the time while managing a family of five was overwhelming her.

We spent a good deal of time working with Tabitha and John to craft a balanced and equitable work map of all the chores in their household. When we finally came to what seemed like a fair solution, both of them looked at us and said, "He/she won't hold up his/her end of the deal." We had just wasted several hours only to discover that there was much more to the story. Although John and Tabitha kept arguing about household chores, there was a whole lot bubbling beneath the surface, including attitudes toward gender roles, definitions of what constitutes "clean," alpha-dog issues, trust, respect, fairness, and various idiosyncrasies of the couple's unique culture.

After we shifted gears, we began the work of deconstructing the conflict by asking John and Tabitha about their families of origin. We found that John had come from a single-parent home with five siblings. Mom worked two jobs outside of the home, and the house was generally left a mess. Tabitha concurred. Not much had changed; her mother-in-law's house was still messy, but there was plenty of love in that home. When we asked John why he had such different standards for his own home, he said, "I never want my family to grow up in that kind of environment. I was always embarrassed to bring my friends home, so I stayed kind of isolated. I vowed to never have this kind of home if I could help it." Tabitha had never known this about her husband; she thought he was just being critical, with a helping of OCD on top. We then asked Tabitha the same question and found that she'd grown up with her mom and stepdad until their divorce and then with her single mom. After the divorce, Tabitha's mom struggled to finish her education and then went on to get a great job in the design field. Tabitha's home growing up was tidy, and Tabitha took part in keeping things orderly. In her mind, she was doing her job at home by keeping the house tidy, so when John complained about a closet or a cabinet being messy, she told him she would address it, but then forgot about it because she never took it that seriously. Tabitha was on a track to eventually fire herself from the stay-at-home-mom job, hire a housecleaner, and work to develop her writing career. She explained that she got to "good enough" with the housework and then turned her focus to her writing. When she shared this, she actually started crying. Tabitha's creative desires were very dear to her, and she wanted John to care about this part of her heart. John did not realize that Tabitha had ambitions beyond supporting him in his career; he thought of her writing as a hobby. When he saw her tears, he was able to understand more clearly just how important this was to her. When Tabitha and John got married, Tabitha was very supportive of John's dreams and wanted to start a family, so she kept her dreams on the back burner, until now. Now, all of a sudden, housework was keeping Tabitha from her dream! It was the enemy! Well, with these and many other layers peeled back, we were able to get at some tender core issues: John's anxious reaction to his perception of a messy house and the fear that it brought up in his and Tabitha's private ambitions. From there we were able to negotiate space and time for both needs, no matter how small or large, without judgment. Both John and Tabitha learned to respect each other's underlying issues and not just tolerate each other's idiosyncrasies. When each of them revealed their vulnerable side, they found that they truly cared about each other's happiness. You see, it wasn't enough to come up with a work map; we needed to reveal their hearts. Once we did this, the work map fell into place.

Jim's Story

Elizabeth generally keeps a very clean house, and I am a very neat person who always puts away what I take out. Our teenage daughter is another story; she sees no value whatsoever in having a clean house, particularly her bedroom (see chapter six on parenting). When Elizabeth and Olivia get together to cook, it looks like a tornado came through the house, and they are both as happy as can be. Not so for Papa Bear. It drives me crazy when the house is a mess.

Anyway, conflict erupted after one of Olivia and Elizabeth's food celebrations. They cooked dinner and had fun, and as the night wore on, simply went to bed and left the kitchen a mess. I woke up the next morning to go to my office and was angry. To me, cleaning up after yourself is a matter of respect for others, right? I felt that by leaving the kitchen a mess, Olivia and Elizabeth were being disrespectful to me.

After, ahem, a discussion, I came to realize that I had some very traditional ideas about a woman's role in the home. I always pictured a genteel Southern housewife gifted in all things domestic (who also happens to be on TV!). Elizabeth, on the other hand, had come into the marriage as a hard-driving career woman who'd hired people to clean house. All we can say is that we're still working on this, but when I go out of town, Elizabeth and Olivia sometimes get completely crazy and actually leave dirty pots in the sink. Overnight! Ughhh!

BOOT CAMP CALL TO ACTION—WITH YOUR MATE

Think about your attitude and your mate's attitude toward chores. Don't judge and don't try to resolve any differences in attitude; remain open and curious about the differences. As you work through the following questions, make no comment other than "That's interesting. I didn't know this about you." Write down the answers to the following questions:

- What would your home look like in a "clean" state?
- What is your definition of the role of a good wife/ husband?
- What is your attitude toward leadership in marriage? Should it be shared, husband led, wife led, or vary depending on the situation?
- What percentage of the household work should each party contribute?

The answers to any one of these questions may lead you in a different direction than the issue of chores. Take your answers to these questions, open up a dialogue, and try to "peel the onion." The question always to be answered is "What are we really fighting about?" Workload will definitely be a part of the answer, but if the issue is respect, gender roles, leadership, or the definition of "clean," start there. Always deal with the deepest issue first. We often find that when deeper issues are cleared up, the negotiation of a household work map becomes much less arduous.

If you have gone in a completely new direction from the discussion of chores, read chapter five, Personality Differences, and chapter eight, Fighting. This book is chock-full of ways to deal with deep issues! If you still find that there is conflict regarding chores, then continue reading.

Housework sucks, and unless you're fortunate enough to have a housekeeper, it's going to continue to suck. No one wants to come home from working all day and clean. No one wants to juggle kids, errands, cooking, laundry, and doing the dishes in addition to cleaning the entire house. Even if you don't mind doing these things, you can easily and quickly burn out if it becomes your daily (unpaid!) duty. Ideally, each person in the household would pick up after themselves without being told, and all chores would be done peacefully and quickly with the help of merrily chirping little birdies. That's not going to happen. So what do you do about it? You do what you do in every other area of your life that is successful: You make a plan.

Simply put, if you fail to plan, you're planning to fail. Without an explicit agreement, daily chores can lead to conflict in marriage, becoming an all-out battle, or at least a source of daily tension. So, it's important that we get this right!

First, we're going to consider various styles of task management. Note that each style can be equally effective. All you have to do is identify which one is a good match for you and your mate. Often couples get into conflict because they don't realize that they have two different perspectives on doing chores.

Luckily for us, a team of UCLA researchers did the work of watching dual-income couples prepare dinner together, a very common task. They found that there are basically four different task-management styles among spouses:

- Silent collaboration: Partners work together on the task without directly speaking.
- One partner as expert: One spouse assumes authority over the task and respectfully guides the other spouse's contribution.
- Coordinating together: Partners work in harmony, verbally organizing the effort.
- Collaborating apart: Partners accomplish their assigned tasks in separate physical spaces.

Obviously, if you're both wrestling for the role of expert leader, or you're a silent collaborator while your mate is waiting for directions, you're going to run into problems.

Jim and Elizabeth's Story

It probably comes as no surprise to anyone reading this book that we both consider ourselves to be experts. We're not the kind of couple who's going to coordinate together or collaborate apart. As a result, we have to be very intentional when we work together and decide ahead of time which one of us will assume authority over the task (based on who is better at it, not by gender) and which one of us will be in a supporting role—and stop being a bossy pants.

BOOT CAMP CALL TO ACTION—WITH YOUR MATE

Discover Your Style

Discuss each of the interactive styles with your mate and identify which one of the styles best describes you and how this impacts your household chores.

Distribute Chores

A marriage that allows each person to contribute depending on his or her specific skill set is a win-win environment that cultivates a supportive and respectful marriage. This is one instance when your differences will provide strength to your marriage, so take advantage of it! Don't worry about cutting the list in half and making sure each person has an equal number of assigned tasks—be realistic, knowing that some tasks are more time-consuming than others.

Try These Steps:

1. Assign appropriate chores. Resentment will be at an all-time low if each person has a job that they are good at doing and/or enjoy. Chores that no one wants to do, such as cleaning the toilet, can be traded off every month.
2. Get everyone involved! Everyone who contributes to making the mess should be contributing in some way to cleaning it up. Even if monitoring and assisting the younger ones seems to take more time than if you just did it yourself, it's important to get your kids in the habit so that one day they'll be a good partner to their spouse!

3. Stop keeping score! "Encourage the effort, or embrace the task," says Alan Hawkins, a family studies professor. "The same woman who complains about her husband also gatekeeps." That is, she critically supervises the domestic efforts of her husband. If you're gatekeeping, consider your partner's feelings. What's true of kids is also true of adults. If you hand someone a task and then hover and criticize, no one will want to do that task again! It's demoralizing, and certainly demotivating.

4. Chore agreements are not tablets from on high. If at any time you feel that the division of labor isn't working, simply have a conversation and adjust accordingly. Effective plans are realistic plans!

5. Get it done. Be your own motivator. No one wants to nag, and no one wants to hear nagging. This is everyone's responsibility. Don't sit around waiting to be prompted. Now that you have a new perspective, you have communicated with your spouse about what each of you would like to do or is good at doing, and you have made a plan, just do it! Cleaning is not always going to be fun. There is not always going to be time to crank up the music and burn those calories, but it is a necessity to a healthy life. A clean and well-ordered home allows your relationship to thrive.

6. Compliment each other! A positive and rewarding environment is a productive environment. A study done at UCLA concluded that a sense of being on the same team and unity between spouses is critical to having a healthy,

happy home. A hardworking heart is nurtured by verbal appreciation. Honor each other for your efforts.

BOOT CAMP CALL TO ACTION

Now is the time to put what you've learned into practice. First, get into a dyad with your mate; that is, sit facing each other, knees to knees, making eye contact. During this drill, you will be having a frank discussion with your mate. Remember Boot Camp Rule #1—when one person is talking, one person is listening. No exceptions!

- Encourage your mate by telling them that you want to serve him or her by sharing the responsibilities of running the house and why.
- Cocreate a list of all chores; be sure to include in your list all of the child-centered chores, such as bathing the children/washing their hair or making them lunch in the morning.
- Discuss what chores you enjoy doing. Tell your mate what it looks like to have this particular chore done well. Ignore stereotypical gender roles. There's no reason for the wife to do laundry or the husband to mow the lawn if she enjoys being outdoors and he's happy folding laundry while watching sports.
- Discuss what chores you despise doing. Tell your mate what it looks like to have this particular chore done well.

Now comes the heavy lifting. Just like with money, you're going to put together a kind of budget. Cocreate a list of all chores. Be sure to collaborate on frequency and, again, discuss each chore and define "clean" for each other. You might mean everything in its place and out of sight while he means not that many piles on the floor. One person might want the floors mopped every day while another thinks that can be once a week. Now, divide your list and work together to take on specific chores based on whatever criteria the two of you decide to use: likes/dislikes, skills, difficulty, time requirement, etc. If one of you enjoys cooking and the other hates it, there's no need to "be fair" or "divide it equally."

Make a commitment to stick with the plan for at least one week, or better yet, one month. Remember, new behaviors and new habits take time to get established. After that, if it doesn't seem to be working out, just make adjustments.

John and Tabitha's Story Continued

In the case of John and Tabitha, they'd never tried to establish a household responsibility or chore system that was satisfactory to both of them. You see, they were stuck because there were some underlying issues that got in the way of crafting a working model of chores. Once they were able to share their hearts, their fears, and their dreams, they were able to get at the chore list. With our help, they created a list of things that needed to get done and decided who would do them and when. And when it didn't all work out exactly as they'd thought it would, they revised the plan to accommodate their real needs. They now reevaluate the list every couple of months and often catch themselves having skipped the "shared" chore of cleaning the garage. Laughing about it, they choose a weekend to work their butts off together and plan a celebration dinner for Sunday evening to celebrate all that was accomplished.

KEY TAKEAWAYS FOR THIS CHAPTER

- Managing chores is one of the top causes of conflict in marriage.
- Managing chores is often just the tip of the iceberg, with the real issue below.
- Identifying your attitudes about chores and communicating them to your mate is one of the first steps to effectively managing them.
- Clarify your task-management style for your mate and be willing to adopt different styles as needed.
- Creating and maintaining a chore management system is one of the best ways to have a happy home.

5

PERSONALITY DIFFERENCES

QUICK QUIZ

Do you feel that your mate just doesn't get you? Does your mate talk and talk and talk, or say absolutely nothing? Does your mate seem to look at the opposite sex too much? Does it seem like your mate never wants sex or always wants sex? Does it seem like your mate is overly dramatic or rarely shows emotion? Is your mate the life of the party or a wallflower? If you feel dissatisfied in any of these areas, the tools in this chapter will help you better understand why you do the things you do and why your mate does things differently.

Jim and Elizabeth's Story

So, to answer the question we are often asked: Yes, we fight too, and this one was a doozy. Working together can be stressful, but working fifteen-hour days for fifteen days straight nearly put us over the edge. After spending all this time using our

Boot Camp tools to manage our clients' conflicts, we noticed that we weren't getting anywhere in our own relationship using these tools.

With the help of a trusted colleague, we were able to see that there was a pattern at play, a dramatic difference in the way that we manage stress. When Elizabeth gets stressed out, she cancels as many nonessential activities as possible, gets very quiet, and tries to conserve energy. She also likes to engage in philosophical, brainiac conversations, like how do we solve the problems of the universe. When Jim gets stressed out in situations like this, he recharges his batteries by being social, playing cards, and joking and moving around a lot as a way of staying alert. He does not like to engage in think-tank activities; he just wants to keep it light. Jim also likes to have sex when he's stressed out, and Elizabeth? Not so much.

His stress-management strategy was stressing Elizabeth out! So she criticized him. She told him to calm down and distanced herself from him as much as possible. As a result of that distancing, Jim then felt rejected and became even more aggressive in his pursuit of her attention and time, which caused her to run even faster and farther away.

We finally realized that we were behaving in a completely normal way based on our personalities. Elizabeth is an introvert, someone who conserves energy and becomes passive when exhausted. Jim is an extrovert and a man and uses activity and aggression when under stress or while problem-solving.

VIVE LA DIFFÉRENCE!

Through years of Marriage Boot Camp seminars, we've found that relationship problems can often be traced to the differences in our gender traits, our personalities, or the way we process information. While our differences can make us extremely attractive to one another, differences can also be at the root of our dissatisfaction. Being aware of some of the basic differences between you and your mate is a tremendous help in overcoming difficulties. We want you to better understand each other's basic wiring so that you are better able to manage your ABCs. Remember, when an *action* takes place, the *belief* will drive the *consequence*. Once we understand and learn to accept our essential differences, we can stop judging and trying to change each other—and even learn to celebrate the ways that we complement each other.

THE DIFFERENCE BETWEEN MEN AND WOMEN

So how are men and women different? The most obvious observation is that men's bodies are different from women's bodies, right? In the same way that our bodies are different, so too are our brains.

A 2013 University of Pennsylvania study on brain connectivity revealed "striking" differences in the brains of men and women. Researchers analyzed close to one thousand brain scans and found that the brain circuitry between men and women is very different in ways that used to be laughed off as stereotyped. For example, women are better interpersonally than men, while men tend to be stronger on focused tasks and mathematics.

BRAIN BASICS

Understanding the differences between men and women starts with a basic understanding of the brain. The brain is like a team of experts who each brings their own distinct specialization to the job. Male and female brains each have advantages and disadvantages. The key is to leverage the strengths and compensate for the weaknesses. All of us have to do that in our daily lives, but we can also do that in our relationships.

The brain is divided into two hemispheres and each side has certain strengths, but both sides are needed for the brain to be fully functional. Very broadly speaking, the left hemisphere is the center of logic and houses language and verbal skills. The right hemisphere is the creative and emotional center and deals with abstract thinking and visual-spatial information. The connective tissue between the hemispheres is called the corpus callosum, and this is where many of the differences between men and women begin. Right smack in the center.

In utero, female brains are flushed with estrogen hormones, while male brains are bathed in testosterone. The result of this hormone bath can be seen in the corpus callosum. The corpus callosum in women is thicker than in men. This enables women to use both sides of the brain simultaneously and offers a significant benefit. A woman can quickly come up with solutions to problems using all of the available data in her brain—facts, history, and emotional impact. She can also multitask more efficiently than most men. The downside, however, is that a woman can be easily distracted, can take longer to come to a conclusion, and often cannot tell you how she came to that conclusion. A woman's brain is like a computer, where much of the processing is hidden from the naked eye.

On the other hand, the testosterone bath the male brain undergoes has the effect of destroying some of the right-left connections in the corpus callosum, which slightly diminishes the interconnectivity between hemispheres. The benefit is that a man is able to zoom in on certain kinds of tasks, stay very focused, and work quickly, unburdened by emotional information that can muddy the water. A man can also tell you exactly how he got to the solution that he came up with, much like an adding machine will give you a printout with every piece of information that went into the final calculation. The downside is that emotions and some of the context might be left out of his decision-making.

Women use both sides of the brain for visual and verbal processing and to respond to emotional experiences, while men use the right side of the brain for spatial skills and the left side for verbal skills.

Within the midbrain is an almond-shaped set of neurons called the amygdala, sometimes called the animal brain. The amygdala is the seat of our most basic, unfiltered emotions, particularly fear, pleasure, and aggression. The larger the amygdala, the more aggressiveness. This structure is one of the most clearly differentiated between men and women. A man's amygdala is significantly larger than a woman's and is more active on the right side, while a woman's smaller amygdala is more active on the left. This may help to explain why men tend to respond to stress with action (they fix things), while women tend to respond with thought (they ponder and talk about things).

We like to compare the male brain to a well-organized garage. Everything is in a box, the boxes are clearly marked, and each box is separate from every other box. A woman's brain, on the other hand, is more like a mass of Christmas lights; everything in a woman's brain is connected, and if one of the lights goes out, the whole array of lights is affected.

SOME OF THE DIFFERENCES BETWEEN THE MALE AND FEMALE BRAIN

- A man's brain is eight to ten percent larger than a woman's brain.
- Men's brains, on average, produce more than fifty percent more serotonin than is produced in a woman's brain.
- Men, on average, have a thousand percent more testosterone than women.
- The male brain has a complex visual circuitry that causes men to always be on the lookout for fertile mates.
- Men have a larger dorsal premammillary nucleus and amygdala, which causes men to be territorial and have a more highly developed alarm system for threats against their turf.
- Men have been shown to excel in what is called visio-spatial processing.
- In men, the area of the brain devoted to sexual pursuit is two and a half times larger than this area in the female brain.
- Women have far more estrogen than men, which causes women to be natural "nurturers."

- A woman's brain is much more active than a man's brain. The mirror-neuron system is larger in a woman and causes her to be more naturally in sync with others' emotions and able to read nonverbal emotional cues.
- Women have more activity in the hippocampus area, the part of the brain that stores memories.

Sexuality

There are indeed differences between men and women with regard to sexuality. As you saw above, men are wired for pursuit, initiation, and competition because their bodies are flooded with testosterone. Women are wired to respond; their bodies are filled with estrogen, and that makes them natural nurturers. All of these differences boil down to this simple fact: Men want sex as a physical release and a means to connect, while women desire connection first and from that sense of intimacy will express themselves sexually.

With all of these glaring differences challenging us, what's a spouse to do? For a more in-depth discussion, see chapter two on how to handle conflict over sex.

Conflict Management

All of the scientific evidence points to a major difference between men and women: Men want to *solve* problems and women want to *process* problems. The impact of this difference cannot be underestimated as it relates to conflict management, as we'll discuss in chapter eight. Apply what you learn about the differences between the male and female brain in this chapter to the chapter on conflict when you're working on those steps in your relationship.

Communication

Our very different brain configurations will certainly affect how well we communicate. For a woman, information is integrated with emotion. Her thoughts spring from her head, grab hands with her heart, and pour out through her mouth. A man's thoughts spring from his head but then stop in one of his little compartments. Emotion is sent to a different compartment, while an action or response is generated separately. (Emotions can be brought into play when desired, like when he gives a gift.)

Men are often accused of being unemotional, but the truth is, they just don't show it as readily. His powerful analytical brain responds very differently from a woman's. While a woman's brain will settle on a feeling and allow it to sit, a man's brain is racing to find a way to resolve the feeling and get back to a neutral setting as quickly as possible.

We see this in the common complaint from women that their man doesn't listen to her problems. In fact, he's working very hard to solve her problem and alleviate her pain quickly.

When a wife comes home from work and wants to vent about her day, she's usually not looking for solutions to her problems. She has it all under control, but complaining relieves some stress. She needs to express her emotions to process her day. Because a man is wired to look for solutions and act upon them quickly, he tends to butt in and offer advice, unwittingly triggering arguments. She just wanted him to listen, not to fix it. But he can't help the way he is wired.

Stress

Here's another difference between men and women. The 2013 University of Pennsylvania study found that men are able to think about absolutely nothing; their brain activity can actually flatline. No, really. They can do that. In contrast, women's brains never stop. How many times have you heard a woman joke about wishing she could "turn off her brain" during times of serious stress?

This explains why men and women handle stress differently. When a man gets stressed out, he often wants to slow his brain down and unwind. The last thing he wants to do is talk. For Jim, this means either watching a movie or clowning around. When a woman gets stressed out, she *has to talk about it*, because if she doesn't, her brain feels like it will explode. For Elizabeth, a quiet, intellectual processing session is in order.

Kimmie and Ben's Story

When they first met, Kimmie and Ben both had high-stress jobs working on political campaigns, and with all their common ground, they hit it off. They were married by the time the next election cycle came around, and Ben took a job on Capitol Hill while Kimmie went back on the campaign trail, traveling at least half of every month and bringing home loads of work each night. A couple of times a week, she went out with the staff after work and had a few cocktails before coming home. It was the same way she'd managed her stress during previous campaigns.

Ben was really irritated that when his wife could have been home spending time with him, she was choosing instead to hang out with the same people she'd just spent all day with. Even while campaigning, he'd never been one for cocktailing after work, preferring instead to go home and zone out in front of a basketball game on TV or to bust out the video games and forget his day. That was how he managed his stress. But to relieve *her* stress, Kimmie needed to talk with the people who had shared her stressful day. Kimmie interpreted Ben's complaints about her going out as jealousy that she was still in the campaign game. She suspected he even resented or blamed her for his decision to take a steady job that provided health insurance for both of them.

After going through Marriage Boot Camp and learning about the differences in how men and women process stress, Ben was far more understanding of Kimmie's need to socialize after a rough day at work. And Kimmie let go of the resentment she'd felt about Ben's reaction. He simply didn't understand what she needed in order to relieve her tension because it was so different from what he needed. By understanding how each of them managed stress, they were able to move forward with new strategies for compromise in their relationship.

Personality Differences

In addition to the differences in the physiological makeup of men and women, within each gender there are vast differences in our personalities.

Sheila and Will's Story

Will was in medical school, and he'd always come home from work excited to share with Sheila about his day. But a few years into their marriage, Sheila felt like they weren't communicating anymore. The change seemed to come almost suddenly, but she didn't know what was causing it. She wondered if Will was cheating, but given the hours he was working at the hospital as an oncology fellow, it really didn't seem like a realistic concern. She tried to figure out what she'd done to make him stop talking to her. If he didn't shower and dive directly into bed when he finally got home, he would park himself on the couch and watch stupid television shows, pausing the episode every time she spoke, as if she were annoying him.

What we learned when they came to Marriage Boot Camp was that Will had been struggling more with this particular residency than he had in previous residencies and that he'd lost more patients than ever before. He was having trouble processing everything that happened in the course of a day, and when he got home, all he wanted to do was shut down. Using the male ability to literally flatline his brain, Will was taking care of himself emotionally, but Sheila didn't understand what was going on at all. Once he opened up to Sheila about the difficulty of seeing patients die, not only did she better understand what her husband was going through, but she stopped making the problem about herself. They left with a plan of how to share and communicate better when Will was having a particularly rough day so that Sheila would know when she needed to give him space and not take it personally.

TAPES: TEMPERAMENT, ADAPTATIONS, PASSIONS, EXPERIENCES, SPIRITUALITY

Differences between you and your mate can be broken down into the five facets of personality. At Marriage Boot Camp we use the acronym TAPES to help us better understand the differences between you and your mate when we consider personality. What is your innate temperament? How have you adapted to life in ways that may not have come naturally? What are you passionate about? What kind of experiences have you had? What are your spiritual beliefs? What are the "tapes" playing in your head, the old beliefs that unconsciously affect our beliefs and behaviors? As we've said before, awareness is the first step in managing our innate differences.

Temperament

Temperament describes traits that you were born with; these traits are not likely to change. One of the most obvious differences in temperament is between the introvert and the extrovert. Psychologist Carl Jung first described introversion and extroversion as a difference in energy. Simply put, the extrovert charges his batteries when he's around people while the introvert charges his batteries when he has time alone. Contrary to popular thinking, both the introvert and extrovert can be outgoing, and both the introvert and extrovert can also be shy. If you've ever found yourself asking the question "Why does my mate act like that?" temperament may give you some answers. Any combination of temperaments can make a good match, as long as you manage your expectations accordingly. The classic test for determining temperament is the Myers-Briggs Type Indicator® (MBTI), which is described in detail in chapter six.

Information-Processing Differences

Within the Myers-Briggs Temperament Indicator®, one of the variables is how we gather information. This may seem wonky and irrelevant, but we have seen a lot of conflict in relationships because we often judge each other as doing things the right way or the wrong way. How we perceive the world is not universal and is tied to how our brains are utilized. This construct comes from the study of learning styles in the educational system. It is relevant to our conversation about how to have a happy marriage because understanding your own and your mate's unique tendencies can help us embrace the differences that we find in each other.

According to the Dunn and Dunn Learning Styles Model, developed in the 1960s by professors Rita and Kenneth Dunn, most people are either global or analytic thinkers.

A global perceiver sees the big picture, while the analytic perceiver focuses on the parts that make up the whole. The analytic perceiver believes you have to get the parts clear and all lined up to eventually understand the whole, while the global perceiver claims there's no point in clarifying a detail if you can't see where it fits into the whole picture. If you are a global conversing with an analytic, you may get frustrated by how much information you are being given before the punch line. If you are an analytic perceiver, the global's flimsy level of detail may frustrate you. One might judge the other as either overly talkative or lazy and superficial. Neither is an accurate appraisal.

Adapting to Your Mate's Different Style

Here are some examples of how you can adapt to someone else's style:

- The analytic talking to a global can start with an overview and then ask for patience while he parses the details, always checking in to be sure that he's not frustrating the other.
- The global can make sure that he's giving the analytic enough detail and check in to make sure he's not frustrating her.
- The analytic can think through (as opposed to talk through) and sift out unimportant details when addressing a global.
- The global can add pertinent detail and be sensitive to the analytic's need for information.

What does this actually mean in real-people speak? It means that if you and your spouse are different types of thinkers, it's important to acknowledge your differences and explore them. That way you know how your mate processes the things you tell her and how she processes things that happen to her.

It also means that when you sit down to have a serious conversation, you work as a team to translate each other's unique language, which interprets how the person is feeling. We've been learning throughout this book how different two people can be—well, now you know there's scientific proof that men and women process pretty much everything differently. Armed with that information and the desire to work as a team, patience and compromise can help resolve just about any conflict. The key is: DON'T JUDGE!

Quick question: Which category, global or analytic, do you fall into? This would be a great time to do some journaling and self-discovery. Write down all of the ways that you navigate life as either a global or an analytic and share this with your mate. Ask your mate which category he or she falls into and ask for examples. Discuss how your unique information-gathering tendencies work for you and work against you.

Adaptation

Adaptation describes skills, attitudes, and behaviors that have been acquired in order to function better. These are skills that do not necessarily come naturally to you; you had to train yourself to be good at them. A habit of punctuality, for example, is difficult for many people to cultivate, but it is almost always necessary if you want to have a happy and successful life. Adaptability is essential in relationships. As we learned in our study of the brain, nurturance does not always come as naturally to men as it does to women;

however, both have to be nurturing in order for their relationships to be healthy. The same is true of aggression. It comes more naturally to men—but put a woman's child in danger and you will see her aggression come into full bloom. Adaptation is essential in relationships and will challenge you to grow beyond your own self-interest to consider the needs of your mate. For example, the neatness of your environment may be very important to you, but if you're married to someone who doesn't care about neatness, you will have to adapt. Or follow the steps for conflict resolution and attempt to reach a livable compromise.

Passion

Deep inside each of us are our heart's desires. These desires, these passions, make us who we are. Our dreams motivate us and energize us. Nothing bonds us more than a shared passion, whether for our children or for our life goals. Nothing breaks us harder than having our dreams diminished, ignored, or dashed. In happy marriages, partners value and adopt each other's dreams. Sometimes two people's dreams are in conflict. Think of political marriages in which one spouse basks in the limelight while the other hates campaigning or living in the public eye. Sometimes such couples adapt, and other times these fundamental differences are too great to make the marriage work.

Experience

Experience describes your history. Have you experienced parental divorce, abuse, or neglect? Were you raised in an extremely wealthy family or an extremely poor family? Have you struggled with substance abuse or financial reversals? Do you have an extremely demanding job or work that's unsteady? Differences in experiences can be attractive; you might find a person who has traveled the world fascinating. But differences can also cause distance between you, especially if your mate cannot relate or empathize with a painful past.

Spirituality

Your spiritual foundation is an important factor in relationships. Are you religious? Are you Christian, Jewish, Muslim, Buddhist, nonaffiliated, atheist? Do you consider yourself spiritual? Many couples of different spiritual or religious outlooks happily coexist, but for others it can be a source of conflict.

Our TAPES make us who we are. If you're lucky, your mate's TAPES are either similar and charming, or different but complementary to yours. If not, you can expect that there will be conflict. Self-awareness and mate-awareness, without judgment, is part of what makes relationships happy and healthy. Now is your opportunity to dig into this topic to improve your relationship.

BOOT CAMP CALL TO ACTION

It is now time to self-evaluate. Get out a piece of paper and make a list.

1. Identify your specific gender-related characteristics and those of your mate.

2. Identify your TAPES. A good place to start is to find a Myers-Briggs Type Indicator test on the Internet and take one of the many free assessments.
3. Identify whether you are a global information processer or an analytic information processer.

Engaging Your Mate

This is where the rubber hits the road. Understanding the basic differences between you and your mate removes a lot of anger, resentment, and frustration. It's the key to having a fully satisfying relationship.

MARRIAGE BOOT CAMP QUICK SCRIPT

Approach your spouse with the results of your own fully orbed personality test, which includes gender differences, your MBTI scores, and how you process information, and say, "I just finished doing an assessment of the unique traits that make up my personality, which includes the differences between men and women and the way we perceive things. It's actually pretty interesting stuff. I was hoping you would take a look at this material, maybe take the personality test, and then we could compare results. I think it would be fascinating to see if we're right about the ways we think we're similar and the ways we think we're different."

Try to make it fun. The exercise can be very entertaining, and you may do some laughing over your results together. Talking about how differently the two of you are wired and how you may not communicate in the same way can be extremely liberating. Sifting through the differences without pathologizing them strips the judgment and criticism out. Now you will be able to determine which ones can be modified and which ones have to be embraced as the unique way that we are each built.

Next have a discussion about the basic differences between the sexes that you've gleaned from this chapter. Ask your mate the following questions:

- What are some specific gender traits that you see in me?
- What specific gender traits do you think are in you?
- How do you think our specific gender traits have affected our relationship?

Armed with this information, you are now ready to have a discussion about the ways that you have been judgmental or critical about traits that cannot and should not be tampered with. This is an opportunity to make amends, to stop judging each other and reconnect.

Now share with your mate the description of the way we process information differently, either as an analytic or as a global.

- Which process do you think better describes you?
- How do you think our differences or similarities affect our relationship?

Did you have an "aha" moment? Did you have a "So this is why we fight" epiphany? If you and your mate have different information-processing styles, go back and read through the "Adapting to

Your Mate's Different Style" section and make a commitment to each other to begin adapting and embracing each other's unique design.

KEY TAKEAWAYS FOR THIS CHAPTER
· ·

- Men and women are different. Do *not* underestimate the impact of this.
- We are all built uniquely. Understand your TAPES and understand your mate's TAPES.
- Stop judging each other.
- Learn to appreciate your differences!

6

PARENTING

QUICK QUIZ — Does either one of you put the kids before your mate? Do you fight over how to raise the kids? Do you have a "his, hers, and ours" blended family? Are you afraid you're turning into your mother? If you said yes to any of these questions, then go refill your drink, use the bathroom, and come back ready to dive straight into this chapter.

> Train up a child in the way he should go [and in keeping with his individual gift or bent], and when he is old he will not depart from it.—Proverbs 22:6

Tonya and James's Story

Tonya and James came to the Marriage Boot Camp with conflict over how to raise their blended family. Tonya brought her two girls, ages fourteen and sixteen, and James brought his two boys, ages seventeen and nineteen, to the new nest. Tonya is a fun-loving extrovert and was quite successful in her business, so for the first time James and the boys could afford to have some pretty wonderful vacations in the new family setting. The boys were thrilled with this new arrangement. Tonya's girls had a little different take on this new blended family. Tonya's girls had always had their mama to themselves and had some adjustments to make, not only making space for the new stepfather but also having to share their mom with two additional siblings. Eventually the boys and Tonya's younger daughter found a way to bond and enjoy one another, but Tonya's older daughter fought the process tooth and nail. Tonya's older daughter managed to create havoc in the family by pitting each of the siblings against each other and against the stepparent. Clearly we had our work cut out for us with Tonya and James at the Marriage Boot Camp. The first thing we did was get them to take a look at their priorities.

The most common complaint we hear at Marriage Boot Camp on the topic of parenting is this: My mate always puts the kids first. Big mistake. If your spouse isn't priority one, then your kids will suffer. Samantha, a friend of ours and a single mom with two kids, was bemoaning the fact that she had met "the one," but since her older son didn't like him, she'd had to call it off. After we broke out of our mouth-wide-open shock, we did something that trained counselors just don't do. We told her she was crazy. After she whined about how important her kids were to her and how she wanted them to be happy, successful adults, we made it clear that they never would be that until she got the kids out of the bubble. The bubble, like in the movie *The Boy in the Plastic Bubble*, is a place of protection for the most vulnerable of children. If that's how you see your kids, you are delusional and maybe being manipulated. Elizabeth taught herself to ride a two-wheeler when she was four years old. Why? So she could keep up with her older siblings and not be left behind. Children will be resourceful if they have to be. We often tell the story about baby chicks hatching from the egg. They struggle and peck for what seems to be an eternity; then, all of a sudden, the shell breaks open and the tiny birdling stumbles out. If however, a well-meaning bystander decides to "help" by picking at the shell prematurely, the chick will end up handicapped. This is also true of our children. If we "help" them too much by twisting ourselves into pretzels on their behalf, we handicap them. If we try to keep them from experiencing frustration or loneliness or failure, we handicap them. If, on the other hand, we model to them a balanced relationship with self and spouse, we set them up to have a secure base upon which to build. While they may complain, children love boundaries and want their parents to be strong, wise, and difficult to manipulate: in other words, *safe*.

David Code, an Episcopal minister, family coach, and author of *To Raise Happy Kids, Put Your Marriage First*, says, "These days, many parents seem to be married to their children instead of their spouses. This creates stressed-out parents who feel disconnected from each other and demanding, entitled kids who act out. Some might become overly dependent on parents as a result of all the attention." Code goes on to say, "Kids end up thinking they're the center of the universe and might act selfishly and manipulatively."

Sex therapist Laura Berman, PhD, agrees and puts it in her couples' guide, *The Book of Love*. "No matter how sacrilegious it sounds . . . you need to put your relationship before your children. A strong relationship provides security for your children and demonstrates how a loving, respectful partnership should be."

If you think your children should be achievement-laden and have only the best, think again. Betsy Brown Braun, author of *You're Not the Boss of Me*, says, "It's almost as if you're failing your kids if you don't lavish endless attention on them." Unfortunately, you're not only putting your marriage at risk but you're stressing out your kids.

Now, we at Marriage Boot Camp recognize that there are seasons of life that cause us to focus on circumstances that don't adhere to a rigid God-Spouse-Kids-Work hierarchy. We like to envision life priorities on a moving wheel. This "wheel of priorities" is dynamic and fluid but strives to always be moving toward balance. If someone gets sick, that goes to the top of the wheel of priorities; if you have a work deadline, that moves to the top for a while. If you are in your twenties, your priorities will be different from when you are in your fifties. The key is this: Always put your spouse and your marriage as a natural priority over your kids. It's actually better for your kids to know that they are being appropriately valued in the scheme of things.

BOOT CAMP CALL TO ACTION

Think about your wheel of priorities. List everything you value and then rank them. For Jim and Elizabeth, in rank order it's:

- Relationship with God
- Relationship with each other
- Raising Olivia
- Jim's business
- Marriage Boot Camp

Next, consider the season that you are in right now. For Jim and Elizabeth, Olivia's needs are at the top of our list, and we have sacrificed (for a short time) to get her life organized.

Make a commitment to your partner to put each other first in priority even if you have to sacrifice for a short time for the sake of a greater need. Here are a few things that you can do to make sure your marriage is getting the attention it deserves:

- Make time every day to touch base, kid-free. For Jim and Elizabeth, it's first thing in the morning before work and school. Most of the time it's only fifteen to thirty minutes for planning and prayer.
- Check in during the day. A quick text or phone call during your busy day says "I'm thinking about you."
- Tell your kids that your mate is an adult and therefore takes priority over them. That's right, put them in their place.
- Show your affection for each other in front of the kids. We're not talking about gross PDA; just make sure that

they have concrete examples of the love you have for each other.

- Spend time without them. Go on date nights and even child-free vacations.
- If you're a single parent, let your children know that you need adult company and that by seeking it, you will not only be taking care of them, but yourself as well. As we always say, there's a huge difference between being selfish and having healthy self-interest, which is good for everybody.

For Tonya and James, this was the crux of the problem. As once-single parents, their guilt combined with their love for their children caused them to have a child-centered existence. When they married, all of the children pushed back at the intruder taking up the attention. Tonya and James juggled with trying to keep the kids in first place while at the same time loving each other. Something had to give, and we didn't mince words. "Either make each other your priority or say goodbye to your marriage," said Jim in his usual blunt, direct manner.

The next thing we had to do was train them to manage this household of different personalities. We introduced them to the three-legged stool of parenting.

THE THREE-LEGGED STOOL

If you're a parent, you'll probably agree that it's the hardest but most rewarding role of your life. At Marriage Boot Camp we call parenting a three-legged stool: It depends on your personal parenting style, your child's temperament, and your child's age, or season of life. Each of the legs of the stool is complex in and of itself, so in this chapter we'll take a thorough look at each.

FIRST LEG—PARENTING STYLE

When we got married, Jim's two sons were already grown and Elizabeth's two daughters were in college and high school, respectively. With one child at home full-time, we discovered that we have different parenting styles. We're both strong, loving, authoritative parents, but Jim leans toward strictness and rules, while Elizabeth tends to be more permissive and concerned about connection. Not surprisingly, Jim had an extremely authoritarian father and Elizabeth was allowed to run free at a very young age. We had to learn how to work with each other's innate differences in order to launch our youngest child into adulthood and continue to parent our adult children in the healthiest possible way.

Self-awareness is always the first step. Psychologists break parenting styles into three types: permissive, authoritarian, and authoritative. A permissive parent is one who puts few demands on the child, tends to be indulgent, and wants to be the child's friend. Permissive parents often engage in negotiations with their children. Authoritarian parents are strong disciplinarians; they are strict and impose many rules. They demand adherence to the rule of law and punish children who don't obey. If asked to explain, the parent might simply say, "Because I said so." Authoritative parents, on the other hand, blend a caring tone with strong limit-setting and a structured home environment. Ideally, every parent would fit that last category. But we don't.

Most parents lean harder in one direction or the other; they are either too permissive or too strict, which can cause conflict between the parents. The good news is that this results in a child who gets a pretty balanced dose of parenting. The worst-case scenario is when both parents lean hard in the same direction; the child will grow up either hating and fearing authority, or having no respect for it at all. It's the responsibility of the parents to strive for a harmonic balance of the two: enough structure to be conducive to growing and learning, but not so relaxed that the child could come to harm by making bad decisions.

You're probably already quite aware of your parenting style as well as your partner's, and you may fight as a result. But we'll help you learn how to blend your styles and compromise in raising your children.

Make no mistake: Children know when their parents disagree over something that involves them. Sometimes they use it to their advantage, knowing who to ask in order to get the desired answer. In divorced or blended families, it's not uncommon for children to play their parents against each other on a regular basis. It can be as simple as managing to acquire twice the necessary wardrobe for a thirteen-year-old, or it could be weeping to one parent over unfair treatment by the other. Some will even act out by stealing or behaving promiscuously to get attention. Whatever the result, the cause of the problem is the lack of coordinated co-parenting by former spouses with different belief systems and parenting styles.

C'mon, that's not a shocker, right? If you and your former spouse had agreed on everything, you would still be married to each other. But knowing that you don't agree on many things should be a warning to you both that you need to get on the same page with parenting.

Whether divorced or married, it's not a bad thing for parents to have different parenting styles. It just shouldn't be obvious enough for children to either take advantage of or be hurt by. Don't fight about decisions regarding your children in front of your children. Your child doesn't need to know that you ever disagreed when the final decision comes down. Always present a unified front. Even if you don't completely agree with the compromise the two of you struck to resolve the conflict, your kids shouldn't know that. If parenting disagreements have escalated to the shouting and screaming point, it's time to take that battle out of the house and into the therapist's office, where your children can't hear you and you have an unbiased third party to help mediate your disagreement. Here are a few Marriage Boot Camp rules of thumb:

- Create a strong foundation of parenting rules and guidelines before you have children. If you haven't done that, it's never too late. The end of this chapter will give you some tools to do just that.
- It's okay to disagree in front of the children (but not about them), as long as they get to see the resolution of the disagreement and not just the battle. Children should be exposed to good conflict resolution so that they will learn from you. If you haven't yet learned to fight fair, then take your disagreement behind closed doors and read the chapter on fighting.
- Don't be afraid to apologize to your children, and don't be too proud to say "I was wrong." If you and your mate break

the rules or do something hurtful to your child, make sure that you take full responsibility and apologize.

With Tonya and James we discovered that they had very different parenting styles. Tonya was the fun-loving extrovert who was always up for a party and tended to be lenient with the children. James accused her of spoiling her two girls and trying to spoil his two boys. James is a quiet, authoritarian parent with a military background, and he raised his boys with a sense of decorum and strict discipline. In the beginning they appreciated the complementarity of their personalities and found that they brought out the best in each other, but now they were struggling to reach an agreement on how to raise the kids.

SECOND LEG—CHILD TEMPERAMENT

Elizabeth's Story

When my firstborn arrived in December of 1989, I thought my heart had burst open because I had never felt such love before in my entire life.

As Ilsa began to grow and develop, she had most of the traits of your typical firstborn: reliable, conscientious, structured, cautious, controlling, and a high achiever.

While she was headstrong and opinionated and didn't sleep through the night until she was nine months old, she was a relatively easy child to raise. She was obedient and a diligent achiever, and she had the benefit of two devoted—albeit divorced—parents. She and I were so similar. I thought I was brilliant and had this parenting thing down! Right. Not so much.

Along came Olivia, nine years later, to teach me some parenting humility. I was forty-two years old and had had infertility issues. When I found out that I was finally pregnant, I thought I had died and gone to heaven.

Olivia arrived one month early and slept through the night almost immediately (we actually had to wake her because she was so tiny and needed to be fed frequently). Olivia was a happy, smiling bundle of joy, good-natured and easy to please, in contrast to her strong-willed, demanding, overachieving sister, who wouldn't let Mommy sleep.

I remember when Ilsa was eighteen months old and decided that she didn't like the way I was sitting on the couch with my legs crossed. She walked over to me, slapped my knee, and yelled, "Don't sit like that!" I was shocked, obeyed her, and then went crying to my therapist. He explained that in order to have a healthy, happy child, I needed to set limits, but not overreact to her negative emotions or worry what she thought of me. You see, children have strong primitive emotions, and we have to model how to tolerate those emotions. If a child is never allowed to express hatred, that natural aggression goes underground. It comes out when they are in a position of power, no longer suppressed by a powerful parent. Imagine a teenager with an underdeveloped "terrible twos" kind of rage and you can see how damaging this can be.

Clearly, I had two very different children who needed very different parenting strategies. What worked with my first daughter was not working with my younger daughter, and vice versa.

TAPES

You were introduced to this concept in chapter five, and now we apply it to the rug rats. TAPES stands for temperament, adaptations, passions, experiences, and spirit—and we're going to tell you how to understand your child in this way.

T—Temperament

Temperament describes an innate style of navigating life. Aspects of your temperament also vary in intensity; lower levels of intensity make for a more adaptable person, while a high level of intensity requires that you adapt to them. The key to parenting according to temperament is to accept your children for who they are and provide an environment that's supportive of their unique qualities. It's also important to help your child understand his or her particular bent and learn when to go with that bent and when to go against it.

Determining what type of temperament your child has is key to being the best possible parent for this particular child. One of the best tests for temperament type is the Myers-Briggs Type Indicator®. You can find several free tests on the Internet if you just search Myers-Briggs, which is exactly what we did.

We decided it would be fun for all of us to take the Myers-Briggs test and found one online. Each of us came away with a four-letter MBTI identity. Elizabeth is an INFJ, Jim is an ENFJ, and Olivia is an ENTP. The differences between our results and Olivia's were eye-opening. We both said, "So that's why she does that!"

Here is what this test tells you about your child in simple terms. Temperament is broken down along four different axes: what social environment you prefer, how you take in information, how you make decisions, and how you prefer to organize life.

■ Is your child an extrovert or an introvert? E/I

Observe and note whether your child is energized after a playdate or social encounter (E) or exhausted and in need of quiet time (I). An extrovert has a deep need for social time with others, and an introvert needs more time alone. Don't confuse being an introvert with being shy. Both introverts and extroverts can be shy or outgoing.

■ How does your child take in information? S/N

This part of your child's temperament will affect the way your child learns. Does your child like to have information presented in an exact and sequential manner? Does your child have a "just the facts, ma'am" kind of attitude? Then he or she is an "S," senser, and joins the ranks of about seventy percent of the US population. Does your child take in information in a more figurative manner, taking in what he sees and looking for meanings, relationships, and inter-pretations? Does your child love metaphors and look at the grand scheme? Is his motto "Close enough"? If so, then according to the MBTI your child is an "N," intuitive.

■ How does your child make decisions? T/F

Is your child cool and logical when making decisions (T)? It's no surprise that about two-thirds of all males fall into the T, or thinking, category and about the same proportion of females fall into the F, or feelings, category. Observing your child's preference will help you and your mate guide your child through decision-making. The T child with a logical bent requires the facts. "Because I said so" is very difficult for this child to hear and comprehend. A child with an emotional bent (F) will need to know how it will feel and how it will make others feel to make a particular decision.

■ How does your child deal with the outside world? J/P

Is your child structured and punctual (J), or spontaneous and easily distracted (P)? A common mistake is to assume that the J (for judging) child is inflexible and the P (for perceiving) child is a disciplinary problem. Yes, having spontaneous children can be like herding cats, but they tend to be creative problem-solvers and cheerfully open-minded.

Tonya and James knew instinctively that their four children were quite unique and different; in fact, they had nicknames like "mini-me" and "Grandpa Smith" for the children because they were so similar to other characters in the family. They just never thought about how this might be affecting the family and how they were to manage the differences. They took a "love them all the same" strategy that many parents believe is the answer, and when we introduced them to the different temperament types and how they all require a slightly different parenting strategy, they were overwhelmed. We wanted to make sure we gave them tools that didn't require an advanced degree in psychology, so we sent them home with a project. We had them create a fun family night and test each person using one of the simple and free online MBTI tests, then read each person's assessment to the group. This is what Jim and I did with our family, and we had a blast. We used the HumanMetrics test, but there are many available. Once each family member got some clarity and awareness about each person's unique design and had some fun with the assessments, we had Tonya and James ask each of the children some easy questions with some Marriage Boot Camp rules: When one person is talking, everyone else is listening. Talk only about yourself, not about your siblings. Don't judge each other. Never use a person's personality traits to tease them.

Here's the question: Based on your type, what can we all do to make your life go smoother? Tonya and James were pleasantly surprised how insightful each of their children was and now had enough information to begin the process of creating a parenting strategy plan together. At the end of this chapter you will find a road map to a parenting strategy so that you and your spouse can have a plan of attack with your children.

What Tonya and James found was that making room for the diversity of their children was not as difficult as they thought. They reconfigured their social schedule to accommodate the introverts in the clan. Before this discussion, Tonya, the party animal, was driving most of their social life, thinking, "Who doesn't love a party?" They found that this was an easy thing to change. They also found that each of their children was at a slightly different stage of life, although they all had a common need for developing their identity. This started a creative vibe between Tonya and James, and they came up with a plan to encourage each of their children to pursue their unique interests—music, sports, and science—and built some family activities around them. Finally, they wrestled with the difference in their parenting styles by coming up with a list of issues in these three categories: no flexibility, some flexibility, and open to the child's preference.

Tonya and James came up with a rock-solid parenting strategy that brought peace and harmony into their home like they had never had before. They still have disagreements about Tonya allowing the kids to stay up and eat ice cream with her, but we will hold that discussion until we get to the chapter on conflict resolution!

A—Adaptation

Adaptation is the tool you need to teach for those times when your child's particular bent is working against her. While we want to honor our kids' unique personalities, it's also our job to prepare them to live successfully in the world, and sometimes that means taming certain traits, at least in certain situations. So rules and manners are important. Parents, you *must* have clear and collaborated nonnegotiables and be prepared to battle together against all of the natural tendencies of your children to make sure that they learn to submit to reasonable authority. If you and your mate go behind each other's backs in disagreement, you are not only harming your marriage, but ultimately you will be harming your children.

P—Passion

It is incumbent upon the parents to observe their children and to discern each child's little heart's desires. These desires—passions really—make them who they are. Their dreams will motivate and energize them. Nothing hurts a child more than being pushed onto a track or path that does not fit. How many parents have mistakenly pushed their artistic sons to play football, or how about the doctor who wants all of his children to follow in his footsteps?

E—Experience

We all want to shelter our children from any kind of harm or negative experience, and frankly, that's our job when they're small. But then there's real life. Children may experience divorce, abuse, poverty, instability, or neglect. They may experience illness, learning difficulties, social problems, or major disappointments. The "E" in TAPES has to be taken into consideration in our parenting strategies.

Michael and Martha came into the Marriage Boot Camp in crisis, devastated by their sixteen-year-old daughter's admission that a family member had sexually molested her. After we dealt with the guilt and recriminations, we dug into the daughter's experience to help the parents deal with it. Their daughter was only eight years old at the time of the abuse and had been "groomed" by her abuser to keep secrets and was threatened with harm and abandonment if she ever revealed anything. The abuser had been out of her life for many years and was no longer a physical threat, but the wounds remained. After alerting the proper authorities, Michael and Martha were faced with the challenge of helping their daughter and their own hearts to heal from this experience. A trained adolescent therapist joined the team, and she brought insight and training, as well as an action plan, to this wounded family. This is just one example of how a unique life experience must be incorporated into the overall parenting strategy.

Each of us has a lifetime of events that affect us and our children and shape the way we parent. There are specialists and programs that can be called on to support you, like divorce recovery for kids and support groups for everything from children with disabilities to grieving children. One organization that we have recommended over the years is Confident Kids Support Groups. Do the legwork on the Internet, with your school counselors, or at your local library. You and your mate do not have to do this alone. Remember, it's not as important to look at what your experiences did to you as it is to look at what you will do with your experiences.

S—Spiritual Foundation

We view human beings as spirit beings with a temporary wrapping of flesh; our flesh dies away, but our spirits remain. What is your personal spiritual worldview? Are you religious? This factor cannot be underestimated in its impact on our children. Whatever your beliefs, teach your children to understand the spiritual aspect of their being.

THIRD LEG—SEASON OF LIFE

The third leg of healthy parenting is knowing that your approach has to change and adjust to the season of your child's life. The way you parent your three-year-old has to morph as he or she enters the teenage years. As their personalities develop, you'll have to adjust your parenting style—as a team—to meet the needs of each individual child.

Let's take a look at Erik Erikson's stages of development as it relates to your child.

Stage 1: Attachment

The first year of a child's life is characterized by dependence. You understand the meaning of sacrificing to the dependence of an infant when you haven't taken a shower in three days and you're exhausted from middle-of-the-night feedings. The way a parent responds to the child's needs, with or without consistency and stability, determines whether or not the child will learn to trust. Your job is to help your child feel safe.

Stage 2: Autonomy

The second stage of a child's life, the toddler years, is characterized by the beginning of independence. This is the stage of the "terrible twos," and we parents need to learn to let go a bit. Toddlers can be allowed to choose what foods they eat and to dress themselves, which gives them the satisfaction of doing things on their own. But it is also a time of frustration (tantrums!) for toddlers who can't do everything they'd like on their own. It is important at this stage to give your children a sense of control over as much of their environment as is practical.

Stage 3: Initiative

Between the ages of about three and five, children begin to develop a sense of self-initiative. This is the time when children begin to experience their internal impulses and are either encouraged to try new things or discouraged and taught to limit their activities and limit risk. Leadership and decision-making abilities blossom during this time. If an overprotective parent or a parent who does not want to be bothered squelches a child's initiative, the result is a child who feels guilty for being a nuisance and will be slow to interact with others. Or the child becomes terrified of doing new things. A guilt-ridden child will also limit risk, which limits their potential. Your job is to encourage your child to try new things in a safer, supportive environment.

Katherine and Ray's Story

Katherine and Ray came to the Marriage Boot Camp because they were having conflict over raising their school-age children. Ray and Katherine thought they were the perfect couple because they shared the same quiet personality and tendency toward introversion and had always gotten along great. They had both been raised in extremely strict and sheltered circumstances and agreed that they did not want to pass on their own resulting struggles with fear and isolation to their children. Katherine, in particular, felt that she had broken free of the bubble her parents had raised her in and was seeing the world from a new perspective entirely. That was fine until she and Ray started having children.

Ray didn't trust the local public school and refused to put their children in a Catholic school, which happened to be the best education available in their price range, because he was a Protestant. Katherine disagreed completely; she felt the Catholic school offered an excellent education and that teaching their faith at home would be sufficient.

The challenge for Ray and Katherine was not just about school choice. It was also a fundamental question about how to raise their children conservatively but without isolating them from the culture. After raging battles about what to do (as raging as two complete introverts can get), they decided to break with the overprotective family tradition they'd grown up in and allow their children to take some risks. They reached a compromise that felt acceptable to both of them. Katherine would homeschool their children but would get them involved in the public school system's extracurricular activities, such as sports and children's theater.

Stage 4: Competence

The elementary and middle school years, between ages six and eleven, are considered to be some of the toughest years in all of life. Social interaction with peers and school activities combine to challenge a child's feelings of success and self-worth. His school and home environment will either engender a sense of competence or feelings of inferiority, depending on the quality of support and encouragement he receives. She will learn to feel confident in her ability to achieve her goals, or will feel inferior and doubtful of her own abilities. The job of the parent is to give your child confidence in their abilities.

Stage 5: Identity

Adolescence brings the critical life challenge of developing a strong identity, an identity that will be the launching pad for finding purpose and direction in life as an adult. This is your final period of active influence. The parents' job during this stage is to encourage exploration. Let your children try on as many hats (or hair colors!) as they want to. This is also a time of "differentiation," when a child needs to feel different from the parent and forges a distinct personality of his own unique design. That's why it's the time of greatest conflict between children and their parents. Many a parent makes the mistake of feeling rejected by his teenager and responds by trying to limit her growth. Pressuring your adolescent into an identity that does not fit her can result in rebellion, negative identification, and feelings of confusion.

Stage 6: Intimacy

Well, your job is done . . . or it should be. The sixth stage of life, between the ages of nineteen and forty, is a time of forming intimate adult relationships. By this time, your adult child should have launched his or her own independent life. Failure in this stage can leave a person feeling isolated and alone. And let's face it, while *Failure to Launch* might have been a funny movie, there's nothing funny about your thirty-year-old sleeping on your couch while you do his laundry.

Stage 7: Generativity

In middle adulthood, our mission is to create, nurture, or give back. This is a time when a person's true sense of purpose plays a major role in determining happiness. We've found our true purpose by serving at the Marriage Boot Camp. In helping struggling relationships and marriages, we find a sense of fulfillment and giving back. A failure to find ways to contribute to society can leave a person feeling disconnected and useless.

Stage 8: Integrity

The senior years, from the age of sixty-five until death, is a time of looking back and assessing your legacy, of asking, "Did I live a meaningful life?" If you answer yes, you will have a sense of peace and fulfillment even in the face of death. For those who answer no, bitterness, regret, and feelings of despair may result. There is nothing sadder than dying with regrets about the way you lived your life and conducted your relationships. It's wonderful to be a powerful politician, a rich entrepreneur, or a famous actor, but when the chips are down and you're getting closer to the light, these accomplishments are not going to be racing through your mind. Remember the adage "Nobody on their deathbed ever wished they'd spent more time at the office." It's true. Your relationships will always be the most important and enduring accomplishments of your life.

BOOT CAMP CALL TO ACTION

Now comes the action—it's time to create a real, solid parenting plan with your mate. Create a parenting strategy that incorporates your and your mate's parenting styles, your child's temperament, and your child's season of life. It is definitely better to do this with your mate, but it can be done on your own if that's the way it has to be. Just make the plan.

Here is an example of a plan that Jim and Elizabeth created together:

Season of Life: Olivia is a teenager, and her core challenge is to develop a strong and healthy identity.

Parenting Styles: While both of us parent with authority, Jim tends to be strict and Elizabeth tends to be more permissive. Knowing this, we must agree on which areas have no flexibility, which have some flexibility, and which can be open to Olivia's preference. And we must discuss matters where we disagree together, separately from Olivia, and present a united front when a decision is rendered.

1. The areas in which we felt no flexibility were attending church, doing chores, completing homework, and behaving morally. We would hold a firm line together on these things.

2. We felt we could be more relaxed and flexible on the actual timing of chores (as long as they got done in a reasonable period of time), allowance and spending money, and schedules and family time. We both acknowledged that as Olivia grew up and got her own life and friends, she wouldn't be home as much and the things we'd always done together would have to change. So we set some fixed family activities in place but agreed to be flexible with the scheduling.

3. We agreed that Olivia had reached the age where she could make her own decisions about food choices, clothing, and extracurricular activities. As long as her choices remained healthy and she cooperated in the areas that were not flexible, we would not intervene even when we disagreed with her choices. The "Olivia's preference" category recognized that our growing daughter was capable of making many decisions for herself.

TAPES

T—Temperament

We measured Olivia according to the MBTI and she is an "ENTP."

E: Olivia is an extrovert who needs plenty of opportunity to socialize. She loves to talk, and talk, and talk. Elizabeth, the introvert, had to make some compromises and find ways to be comfortable with Olivia's energy, like hand her off to Jim at times!

N: Olivia would speak in poetry and metaphors if she could. "Close enough" is her goal. Sometimes this results in doing her homework but neglecting to turn it in! This was an area of frustration for us because neither of us had this habit. Once the trait was normalized for us, we stopped being angry and realized that we had to work on the "A" in TAPES. With Olivia's rich and creative gifts, we came up with a reminder whiteboard designed by Olivia, which hung right outside her bedroom door, with alerts, deadlines, and rules. We also synced up her phone with the same information so that we had several layers of alarms in place. So far, it's working!

Olivia is a "T" (thinker) versus an "F" (feeler). She doesn't understand why we get so angry when she can clearly delineate (often in metaphors) all of the reasons she does what she does. She is more interested in being right than in being liked, and she frustrates her teachers with her continual flow of questions, some with an edge that hints, "You don't know what you're talking about." Her thoughts make perfect sense to her, and she will debate with you all day. Therefore we have to repeatedly talk about her responsibility for her chores, because she just doesn't see the importance. She sees rules as suggestions, to be followed only so far as she deems them relevant to her. Of course, this was a topic of conversation. Once Olivia understood that she had a unique personality that sometimes got her in trouble, she was able to start to modify and adapt. She was living out a Marriage Boot Camp adage, that it was better to be happy (and out of trouble!) than to be right.

Olivia is a "P" (perceiver), as opposed to a "J" (judger) like her parents. She is loath to put a stake in the ground and prefers to keep her options open while her parents live to commit and execute. Because of this, keeping her on time can sometimes be a nightmare. As new information comes in, Olivia often feels a need to adjust course. Another need for discussion! Again, Olivia came to understand her unique trait and clearly understood the risk/reward of being on time or not, of executing an assignment or not. It was amazing to see that with self-awareness (and with less parental criticism) came less of a desire to "do things my way"; she simply weighed the benefits and made much better choices. We also had to make some parenting changes. While we still held her to account, we now did it without shame or anger and communicated our understanding of her innate traits.

A—Adaptation

As parents, we must affirm Olivia's unique design while at the same time teaching her to do things that go against her nature. For example, her natural bent toward "close enough" will create problems for her in areas where exactitude is required. We must help her develop a sense of how others may be feeling and understand the relevance of this skill. We must teach her to be regimented on some things, like punctuality and the completion of tasks by a deadline. And in doing this, we have to be sure to make logical arguments, not emotional ones. Saying "That hurts my feelings" doesn't always compute with Olivia.

P—Passion

We have to pay very close attention to the things that thrill Olivia's heart and guide her toward activities that align with them. It's also our job to be supportive and enthusiastic even when it's not something we would have recommended had she asked our opinion about it. This is the time when she is finding her true self, and she has to be allowed the room to develop her talents, whatever they may be and in whatever realm she chooses.

E—Experiences

Olivia is a child of divorce, and that means recognizing those wounds. In addition to supporting her in working this through, Jim recently formally adopted her, even though she's getting close to adulthood. We hope this helps to solidify the trust and bond he's built with her while helping to raise her.

S—Spiritual Foundation

We must continue to help Olivia grow spiritually by modeling our beliefs, teaching her our beliefs, and exposing her to the spiritual disciplines that are important to us. Our children will ultimately make their own decisions about religion when they grow up, often in partnership with their own spouses, but we have to provide a strong foundation, no matter which route they ultimately choose to follow.

Engaging Your Mate

If you have done most of the heavy lifting on putting together a parenting strategy, this is the time to engage your mate and share your thoughts. Find a time when you're both relaxed and have plenty of downtime and the kids aren't home to overhear or interrupt you. This process can take a couple of hours. Go through each of the three legs of the stool and make sure that you are getting buy-in along the way.

Start with your child's current season of life. It should be pretty straightforward because it's based on age. Be sure to read through the section on your child's season with your mate and understand the developmental needs associated with their age.

Next, share what you've found in researching your child's temperament and TAPES and discuss your mate's views.

Finally, talk about your respective parenting styles and any ways in which these may cause conflict.

MARRIAGE BOOT CAMP QUICK SCRIPT

Parenting is clearly a matter that you and your spouse have to approach together, even if he or she hasn't been willing to engage with you on other relationship issues you may have. If you need help broaching the subject, here is a quick script to try:

"Honey, there's nothing I want more than to have healthy, happy kids and peace in our family. I really want our marriage to be strong, and I don't want the kids to get between us. I want this so much that I got this book with a chapter on how to do just that. There's an exercise on creating a parenting plan. I took a stab at it, but I'd really like to go over it together and get your input."

You can have the best intentions in the world but still not be good parents if you and your spouse cannot get in sync about how to raise your children. You have to evaluate each child as an individual and figure out how to treat them all equally while not necessarily treating them the same. The parenting plan you create together will definitely grow and change as your child progresses through the seasons of life, but by then, adjusting your parenting plan will likely be something you enjoy doing together, as it gives you an opportunity to relive and celebrate your children's successes.

KEY TAKEAWAYS FOR THIS CHAPTER

- Parents should not make the fatal error of allowing the children to be the center of their universe; the two in marriage should take top priority.

- Parenting is a three-legged stool—a combination of parenting style, the child's temperament, and the child's season of life.
- Every person has a set of "TAPES"—Temperament, Adaptations, Passions, Experiences, Spirituality— which affect everything from marriage, to parenting, to vocation.
- Couples must create a parenting strategy that considers each of the legs of the "three-legged" stool. In this way they have the opportunity to be the best possible parents to their children and to protect their relationship from being divided over the kids.

7

CHEATING

QUICK QUIZ

Have you or your partner strayed from your marriage and now you're suffering from the aftermath? Have you and your partner considered an open marriage? Do you suspect that your partner is intimate with someone online or at work? Are you secretly connecting with someone that your mate does not know about? If you answered yes to any of these questions, we've got some serious work to do on your marriage.

THE DESTRUCTIVENESS OF INFIDELITY

Mark and Amy's Story

Mark and Amy had been married for twenty-two years when Mark embarked on his first affair. Mark's mother had recently died and, in his grief, Mark had become depressed and angry. Amy was very critical of Mark's reaction to his mother's death, telling him, "You need to be strong for the family." In fact, Amy was constantly critical of Mark in their everyday life and viewed this as a normal part of marriage. She said she didn't want "to give Mark a big head," so she rarely encouraged him.

Mark tried to hide his tears for fear of being mocked and felt ashamed that he wasn't stronger for his wife and family. The more he shoved his feelings down, the more depressed he became. Then along came Monica, a family friend and neighbor who said she understood how he felt because she had just lost her mother and he could come over and cry with her anytime.

Mark did begin spending time with Monica, and she eventually initiated a sexual relationship. He says he never saw it coming and felt like he couldn't say no without embarrassing her and losing her friendship. The truth is, he didn't want to say no. What started out as a shocking and guilt-filled experience ended up becoming an obsession. Monica filled a huge void for him, and he couldn't get enough.

The affair finally ended because Mark's guilt became too much. He ended up confessing the entire thing to his wife and vowed never to do it again. Amy was devastated and humiliated and responded with anger and contempt. Mark asked for forgiveness, but her criticism and contempt knew no bounds. He tried to make it up to her and accepted her anger as just punishment for his sin, but he was miserable and didn't feel any love for Amy anymore.

Mark tried desperately to white-knuckle it through a miserable marriage, but then he fell off the wagon again. This time it was with a woman who pursued him at his workplace. Sally was much younger than Mark, and she looked up to him and flattered him. Mark was able to share his heart and his pain with her, and his discontent in his marriage became the center of many of their conversations.

"This is often how inappropriate relationships begin," says Dave Carder, author of *Torn Asunder: Recovery from an Extramarital Affair*.

"People move from talking in generalities to more specific things, like 'help me understand my spouse' to even more private issues. This starts a gradual erosion of boundaries and often leads to an affair," Carder explains.

Mark and Sally had a very intense friendship and emotional connection. "If your heart races when you anticipate seeing this person, that is a definite sign there is more to the story than friendship," says Carder. "If you have said or thought to yourself, 'If I weren't married, I would marry this person,' that definitely puts the relationship in a different category. This is often when you see people acting like they are drunk in love."

An affair can be life-shattering. If your mate has been unfaithful, it can leave you feeling angry, depressed, disoriented, even enraged. You may find yourself obsessed with knowing every little detail of the affair. The betrayal and deception can leave you numb or feeling wildly out of control. You may suffer from anxiety, depression, low self-esteem, humiliation, or guilty feelings that you could have somehow prevented it from happening.

This is exactly how Amy felt when Mark confessed to his first affair. She was angry, depressed, and humiliated. She swung between wanting to kill Mark and feeling somehow responsible and inadequate. She was absolutely blindsided because she had always thought they had a great marriage; Amy often bragged that Mark would never leave her or be unfaithful and that they had a great sex life. Amy hadn't considered divorce after his first affair, but after the second? She was done. Unfortunately, by the time Mark dragged Amy to Marriage Boot Camp, she had already begun another relationship and was hell-bent on punishing Mark. Her only reason for attending was to parade Mark's infidelity in public. She was unwilling to look at all the facets that make up the profile of a wounded marriage—it was simply all his fault. We were heartbroken, but we also know that unless both spouses are willing to give one hundred percent, the odds of putting the marriage back together are slim.

If you or your partner has been unfaithful, you are not alone. One in every 2.7 couples is affected by infidelity. According to a published report in the *Journal of Couple & Relationship Therapy*, by the age of forty, approximately fifty percent of all wives and sixty percent of all husbands will have had an extramarital affair.

In the case of Mark and Amy, Mark's affairs had an absolutely catastrophic effect on the family. But at Marriage Boot Camp, we don't consider an affair an automatic marriage killer. If you have two willing partners, a marriage can be rebuilt from the bottom up. And if children are involved, we always recommend trying to repair the relationship. Although being raised in a poisonous atmosphere is even worse, children are profoundly impacted by divorce, and parents have a responsibility to avail themselves of every possible opportunity to re-pair the relationship before they throw in the towel.

CHEATING DEFINED

> Cheating is the act of being sexually unfaithful in mar-riage and, in our opinion, any behavior that takes sexual energy out of the marriage is a form of infidelity. Whether it's flirting, pornography, or sharing too much emotional closeness with someone you're attracted to, emotional infidelity can be as dangerous to your marriage as phys-ical infidelity.

Here at Marriage Boot Camp, we have a pretty encompassing definition of cheating. Contrary to what many think, cheating is not just about sex. People cheat for many reasons, but the most common reason is for emotional connectedness.

In *Breaking Free: Understanding Sexual Addiction & the Healing Power of Jesus* by Russell Willingham, cheaters report that they are looking for friendship and they want to be heard. They want to feel wanted, needed, understood, and important.

Cheating can also be an expression of addiction. Every addict is hurting and wounded and will use sex as a means of avoiding feel-ings of pain, a lack of self-worth, or to fill a void left over from childhood, instead of its proper function: connection with another human being. The saddest part of this "false intimacy" is that it leaves the addict a little emptier than when he started and thus requires an increase in dose—and so begins the cycle of addiction.

Experience has shown that a common thread runs through the lives of addicts: They are lonely to the core. The addict has deep, unmet childhood needs that are mistakenly expressed as sexual needs.

Mark was having all-of-the-above types of affairs. His addictive nature was expressed through many outlets, including hard work, competition, and staying chronically busy with projects. Even though he was quite handsome and successful, he had always felt insecure, lonely and isolated. He was sure that marriage would finally end his sense of loneliness and was sadly disappointed when it didn't. Mark's deep need to medicate his pain, combined with an unhappy and emotionally abusive marriage, made him very vulnerable to straying.

Statistically, infidelity is rare in the first four years of marriage. Our wedding is one of the high points of life. We pledge our undying love and devotion to our spouse, and we make a commitment "until death do us part." We're happy and hopeful; the relationship feels new and our Love Banks are full to overflowing. Then real life happens.

Financial pressures, a demanding job, and however many children later, we find that the honeymoon is definitely over. What were once euphoric feelings of love and being loved have changed over time. Along with joy, commitment, and completeness, we start to feel bitterness, disappointment, and resentment. This change in the dynamics of marriage is normal and can deepen the bond between spouses. But under the strain of life, the negatives can start to overtake the positives, and it's at that point that we become more vulnerable to straying. According to John Gottman, a researcher famous for his book *The Seven Principles for Making*

Marriage Work, there has to be a five-to-one ratio of positive to negative in order for a marriage to remain happy and stable.

In addition to the normal stressors, affairs often happen after a major life crisis such as the death of a loved one, the loss of a job, or a major injury or illness to a member of the immediate family. A major life crisis not only brings a tremendous amount of stress into one's life, but also causes us to reevaluate our lives and start thinking about ways to be happier. An affair can distract us from the difficult realities that we face and can make us happy, at least temporarily. As we saw, for Mark, the major life crisis was his mother's death. Mark wanted immediate relief from the pain of his loss. His mother's death also shook him awake to the fact that his marriage was terribly unsatisfying, and he impulsively grasped at opportunities to find satisfaction.

HOW TO AFFAIR-PROOF YOUR MARRIAGE

The best way to deal with cheating is to get in front of the things that cause infidelity in the first place. Marriage Boot Camp has found several common, and avoidable, themes and attitudes that precipitate an affair. Here are the top three strategies to affair-proof your marriage:

- **Make your marriage the number one priority.** Check your worldview. If you or your mate thinks that cheating is socially unacceptable but normal, that monogamy is unnatural, that all men cheat, then you are at risk. If you come from a family where cheating occurred, then you are more likely to be a cheater or to marry a cheater. This attitude of cheating being a fait accompli seems to crop up every few years in someone's book about how men are like animals and that they should trade out partners every few years. Bunk. Human beings are actually wired for healthy monogamy. How do we know this? Not only does every major spiritual discipline espouse the virtue of monogamy, but science agrees as well. Study after study shows that people in healthy monogamous relationships live longer, are physically healthier, have less depression and anxiety, and are less likely to abuse drugs or alcohol. Do you need more proof that we are wired for monogamous relationships? Statistically, those who are married will earn an average of twenty percent more than their unmarried peers. Commit right now to leave the fantasy of happy singleness or an open marriage behind and get on with the hard work of making your marriage great.

- **Make personal growth a priority.** If you are emotionally unhealthy or immature, then your marriage is at risk for affairs because instead of acknowledging and working on your own issues, you may project them onto your mate and start looking outside for a new and improved model. Ask yourself, do you bring unresolved wounds into your marriage hoping that the marriage will make things better? Did your parents model an unhealthy marriage to you? Marriage will not only *not* make your personal dysfunction better, but it will eventually make it more obvious. You've surely heard about the nagging wife or the overly controlling husband. Well, guess what; both of these annoying tendencies (and many more) are often pointing to character imperfections. Don't wait until your mate points out your flaws, don't get mad when you are called out, and God forbid, don't go looking outside your marriage for someone who will "appreciate" you. Eventually, anyone you allow to be close to you will see the same things. Finding the perfect mate who will finally "see you in the light that you deserve" will never happen if you are unhealthy. Having a mirror to your life set up by having a loving mate is what we call "iron sharpening iron" and is a blessing, not a curse. The statistical benefits to marriage are tied to these sharpening phenomena, but make no mistake; this is a picture of two swords clanging against each other and shaving off the rough spots, making each other sharp and brilliant. Get rid of the chip on your shoulder and deal with your baggage. At Marriage Boot Camp we always say, "If you change and grow, your marriage will change and grow."

■ **Date your mate.** Remember that in the beginning of your love affair, you were very intentional about creating wonderful moments together. You were driven by the feelings of attraction and excitement to be together. Best-case scenario, after years of marriage, your feelings will change from being lovesick to being deeply in love and comfortable with the security and constancy of your mate. The problem is that being lovesick—the butterflies, the preoccupation with your love interest—is actually an energy source that fuels much of the romantic behavior in the beginning and is gone after the romantic phase turns into the deeper, realistic phase of your relationship. The challenge is to exchange the butterflies and obsession with discipline and commitment. Make dating a priority and a discipline. Here are a few ideas:

- **Create a sacred date night.** Do not make excuses about time, money, or kids; plan ahead and make it happen. We can tell you from experience, divorce is costly, time-consuming, and a planning nightmare! Date night can be as simple as a preplanned time to watch your favorite TV show or as elaborate as a food adventure at the hot new restaurant in town.

- **Get physical!** Studies show that couples that are physically affectionate rarely stray. Hugs, kisses, and hand-holding may seem insignificant, but they are found to be powerful glue in a marriage. Having regular, frequent sex also keeps two people focused toward each other and not only strengthens the bond, but also the attraction you have for your mate. Great sex is addictive, in a good way!

- **Create a common interest or hobby.** We have found that most couples get together by means of a common interest, a class, or through work. But after they become a long-term couple, this aspect of their relationship gets tossed aside. Then they complain that they have nothing in common anymore! Find something! Ballroom dancing or serving together to feed the homeless, whatever your interests, find a way to connect.

THREE TYPES OF AFFAIRS

Marriage Boot Camp has found that relationships can survive an extramarital affair, but the ability to survive is affected by the type of relationship the cheater is having outside the marriage. There are generally three types of affairs, and depending on the type, some are more or less difficult to repair than others.

The One-Night Stand

This type of affair usually involves little if any emotional connection and typically occurs when he or she is away on a trip. The prognosis for this type of affair is good as long as it was an isolated event and the cheating mate is truly remorseful. If, however, this is a pattern or, worse, an addiction, then the prognosis goes down. The best strategy is a preventive strategy. Be completely honest about your struggles. Talk about attractions outside the marriage before they are acted on. It is much easier to have this difficult conversation with your mate now than it is to have to apologize for violating your partner's trust later.

The Mistress

This is a real relationship, perhaps a love affair, and can continue for years. The mistress is the plaything, the fun and games, and is relief from the routine and drudgery of life with the job and kids and in-laws. This type of affair is very difficult to recover from but still possible. The cheating mate must be willing to end the relationship immediately and accept full responsibility for the pain he has caused. The cheating mate must rise to a new level of transparency and be open and honest about everything. This may include sharing details about the affair, but be warned—scrub out all of the salacious details. You do not want to create images in your mate's mind that will need to be erased. Share all passwords to any social media sites, the phone, and all financial accounts. The cheated-on partner has responsibility as well and must be willing to forgive and work through this breach of trust alongside their mate.

The "I Want Out" Affair

This type of affair is the worst kind of affair. This is a premeditated move to end the marriage with a deliberately hurtful act. Generally this cheater makes a calculated and premeditated decision to have an affair, knowing the effect will be disastrous on the marriage. This relationship was over long before one spouse decided to engage in an affair. We rarely see this kind of relationship in the Marriage Boot Camp, but when we do, it is often to get help negotiating the split. This cheater has no desire to fix the marriage but would like some help with negotiating a co-parenting relationship with their soon-to-be ex. Very few marriages can come back from this scenario whole, but a working relationship should still be an objective if children are involved.

CAN A MARRIAGE SURVIVE AFTER AN AFFAIR?

Marriages can definitely survive after an affair, but it is hard work. First of all, it has to be clear that the cheating mate is truly remorseful, not just sorry to have been caught. Then, the other spouse has to be able to forgive sincerely and completely. That doesn't mean one and done. Forgiveness is a process that may have to be repeated over and over. The decision to forgive must be a commitment to continue to release the offender every time the pain comes up.

The cheating mate then has to do the hard work of rebuilding the relationship by being a healing agent in the life of his or her mate. The cheating mate is responsible for putting salve on the wound every time the scab gets scratched off. The cheated-on partner must be allowed to talk about his or her pain, while the offender has to be willing and skillful at mirroring back what is being said and felt without being defensive or impatient.

Finally, both parties need to do some digging to find out if the infidelity is the result of a deficit in the relationship or a deficit in one of the individuals.

According to Dr. Mark Baker, there are three things necessary for a healthy monogamous relationship: empathy, a healthy level of closeness, and love. Empathy is the capacity for understanding another person on an emotional level, not just an intellectual level. Healthy closeness is determined by many factors, such as personality or family culture, but in marriage this means that you are able to be apart without being distant and to be close but not enmeshed. Finally, love is defined as a choice to serve your mate and consider your mate before yourself. This is a selfless love, agape love, which puts your mate's interests ahead of your own. Dr. Baker posits that if you can understand your mate on a deep emotional level and have a desire for a healthy closeness to your mate, then this kind of love will be the result.

If there is an identified deficit, both spouses must commit to correcting it. If the infidelity is the function of a sexual addiction, then the addiction and the root of the addiction need to be addressed first. One couple we worked with was devastated by the husband's serial infidelity, which was largely due to a sexual addiction. His commitment to his wife and children was so strong that he checked himself into a monthlong rehabilitation program and continues to walk in accountability, not just to his wife but also to a core group of trusted men. Nothing is too much when your marriage is at risk.

We have found that every affair is a combination of unfulfilled needs and wants with some addictive, self-medicating tendencies. It's rarely just one or the other. As we saw in the case of Mark and Amy, trouble had been brewing for years. This marriage lacked transparency and honesty, which makes intimacy almost impossible. Mark never confronted Amy about her critical spirit because he desperately wanted to avoid conflict. Without this kind of "iron sharpening iron" mirror in their marriage, Amy never realized that she needed to grow. The underlying contempt exhibited by both partners grew and grew and came out in passive-aggressive ways. Unfortunately, the unidentified deficits combined with Mark's unaddressed struggle with sexual addiction made this marriage fail.

WILL *YOUR* MARRIAGE SURVIVE THE AFFAIR?

One of the first questions asked at every Marriage Boot Camp seminar is "Can our marriage survive infidelity?" The answer is a resounding yes! Approximately twenty-five percent of the couples that come to the Marriage Boot Camp are wounded by this one specific marital offense. We reassure them that an affair does not necessarily have to lead to divorce. We've seen couples heal and even strengthen their bond after the devastation, but both parties must be committed to each other and to creating a healthy monogamous relationship, to exhibiting complete transparency, and to avoiding further temptation. Only then can they travel the long, bumpy road to healing and restoring trust.

By commitment, of course, we mean the affair must be over, and the cheater has to take whatever steps are necessary to prove his or her trustworthiness. Both parties must be committed to repairing the damage, rebuilding trust, and engaging intimately with each other.

What do we mean by transparency? This includes sharing details of the offense honestly and openly but without salacious details that could leave mental images with your mate, causing even more harm. It also means giving up a measure of privacy. If you've been watching the *Marriage Boot Camp* television series, you've seen more than one incident of distrust based on one partner's refusal to let the other look at his cell phone messages and calls. This might be tolerable in a healthy marriage, but after infidelity, it's an absolute deal breaker. A cheating spouse who is one hundred percent committed to saving his marriage will willingly give up his privacy to help build a foundation to regrow the trust in the relationship.

The betrayed spouse must also do his or her part and take the job of healing seriously. There will be times of overwhelming anger and despair. These feelings should not be minimized, but it is important to experience these feelings in a way that does not further damage the marriage. Having a same-sex support group, or a great counselor who gives you a safe place to share and talk about your feelings, is a very important part of the healing journey. You cannot do this alone.

The recriminations, however, cannot go on forever. You may mourn what you have lost in your relationship, you may be angry about your mate's actions, and you may feel sad when something triggers the memory of the transgression. But you must also commit yourself to letting it go, a little bit at a time, as your mate works with you to regain your trust.

IF YOU ARE THE CHEATING PARTNER

Much of the burden of healing lies squarely on the shoulders of the unfaithful spouse. You broke the relationship and you have the main burden of fixing it, although you can't do it without the aggrieved spouse's cooperation. You must continue to listen to your mate rage at you, cry about you, and go through the stages of grief he or she requires to become whole again. You can't say "enough already," because that will cause your spouse to believe you don't take your affair seriously enough. In order to be a healing agent in the life of your mate, you have to be completely available to hear her anger and sorrow for as long as it takes. Hear it and then mirror what she says back to her. We have found that if the cheating partner wants his spouse to let go of the pain, then he has to accept his wife's anger without getting angry and fighting back.

"Once it has been determined that a spouse has had an affair, there are four universal concepts you must go through to save a marriage: forgiveness, rebuilding respect, building trust, and building love," Carder says in *Torn Asunder: Recovery from an Extra-*

marital Affair. "Even if you don't stay married, you still need to go through this process in order not to continue to pay the price of the affair in future relationships."

You must view infidelity the way an alcoholic would look at alcohol. There has to be a complete break with any relationships or situations that are a temptation. If the infidelity happened in the workplace, it is our recommendation that you find a way to be assigned to a different department or a different location. If you have the ability and flexibility to change jobs, do it. It's that serious. Your mate will never trust you again when you say you have to work late, and no matter how long it's been since your transgression, he or she will always worry about your behavior on business trips. You destroyed the trust between you, and you must live with those consequences. Removing yourself as much as possible from the situation will mitigate the aftershocks.

HEALING FROM INFIDELITY

Healing from infidelity in the marriage takes time, longer, probably, than it did to build the relationship in the first place. The trust is gone, and it has to be rebuilt, one act of faith at a time. Even if your mate has forgiven what you did, that doesn't mean he or she will ever forget that you strayed.

If both parties make a commitment to follow these strategies with their whole heart, your marriage has a good chance of surviving the affair—and emerging stronger on the other side.

To heal from infidelity, the unfaithful spouse must:

1. **Stop**—The unfaithful spouse must immediately sever all contact with the outside person. This includes not just in-person contact but phone calls, texts, Facebook—*all contact must stop.*

2. **Be completely transparent**—The unfaithful spouse must be willing to answer any and all questions. We have found that open and honest communication about the infidelity leads to greater feelings of connectedness and provides the environment needed for reconciliation. The willingness to communicate openly rebuilds trust. You have to talk about what happened in order to get through it and over it.

3. **Show empathy**—The cheating partner must be empathetic and humble when the cheated-on mate expresses strong emotions about the transgression. Refusing to listen to your mate's feelings and accept that they are real will prevent healing. If you don't let the cheated-on spouse unload the pain he or she is carrying, you will never rebuild the relationship.

4. **Be patient**—Healing from infidelity takes time. The offending spouse should make himself or herself available anytime the pain comes up and be able to listen and mirror back again and again.

5. **Take full responsibility**—Never blame your mate. Show sincere remorse and regret. Apologize every

time the infidelity comes up and assure your mate
that this will never happen again. Express your
commitment to your mate as your one-and-only in
words and touch.

6. **Expect the storm**—Tears, rage, and anger are a
part of the healing process, and you should be prepared to create a safe place for the grief.

—Adapted from *The 7 Stages of Marriage*
by Sarí Harrar and Rita DeMaria

BOOT CAMP CALL TO ACTION

When You Are the One Who Has Been Cheated On

The first thing you have to do if you suspect your spouse is having
an affair is be direct; ask, "Are you emotionally or sexually involved
with someone outside of our marriage?" It is only at the point of
complete honesty that the reparative work can truly begin.

If the honest answer from your mate is yes, three things need to
happen for your marriage to have a chance of surviving.

1. The cheating spouse has to want to repair the marriage.
2. The affair has to stop.
3. You must learn to forgive.

If this cannot happen, then your marriage cannot survive. If your
spouse agrees to number one, then two and three should natu-

rally follow. The two of you will work through the exercises in this section.

But what if you want to repair the marriage and your mate is ambivalent about it? This is a painfully common situation. Here's the secret: At the root, infidelity is a form of disrespect, so it is very, very important that you conduct yourself in a way that inspires respect. Don't beg. Don't whine. Don't threaten dire consequences in the event your mate leaves. Simply share your feelings in a calm manner and communicate that there are limits to what you will tolerate. To quote Dr. James Dobson in *Love Must Be Tough*, "Nothing destroys a romantic relationship more quickly than for a person to throw herself, weeping and clinging, on the back of the cool partner to beg for mercy. That infuses the wayward spouse with an even greater desire to escape from the leech that threatens to suck his life's blood."

The difficult truth is that you must allow your beloved mate to leave you without a fight. The paradox is that when you set someone free, it frequently fans the small spark of love that still exists. All of a sudden, he may begin to recognize that he is going to lose you! If this seems the case, be patient. Work on building your self-esteem, because at the end of the day, your self-worth and dignity will be the cornerstone of your new life without your mate. It is also extremely attractive. Focus on your personal healing and allow the situation with your mate to unfold. When your wayward spouse shows an inkling of interest, that is the time to suggest that the two of you work on rebuilding your relationship with the help of this book.

If your mate is categorically not interested in repairing your marriage, then you must move on. We urge you to make a clean break of it. If a cheating spouse does not want to end the affair, there is no point in trying to save the marriage. It will only hurt you further to fight for what is rightfully yours. Do not beg your mate to love you again; do not surrender your dignity.

Most important, do *not* accept the behavior and allow it to continue for the sake of keeping your marriage intact. This isn't a question of taking a moral stand; if the strategy worked, we'd be for it. In fact, many a desperate spouse has experimented with alternative solutions, but we have never found an alternative to monogamy that works. Open marriages were all the rage back in the late 1960s, when the sexual revolution was at its peak. Yes, that's the answer to cheating! Just say it's okay! Not. Back in 1972, Nena and George O'Neill's book *Open Marriage* spent forty weeks on the *New York Times* bestseller list. They promoted open marriage as a viable alternative lifestyle because the institution of marriage was dysfunctional. By 1977, the O'Neills had reversed their position because none of the open relationships in their study were successful.

Indeed, we have found the opposite is true: Accepting infidelity will only further erode your marriage. There are anomalies, but in twenty years of Marriage Boot Camp, we have not seen any of the creative expressions of relationship achieve the deep, intimate, joy-filled, productive nature that true covenant marriage brings. In fairness, Marriage Boot Camp's philosophy isn't for everyone. We are friendly with several couples who "swing" and have sustained twenty-plus years of stable marriage. Dr. Chris Donaghue, of WE tv's show *Sex Box,* says that he has many healthy, open marriages in his practice, and he is a supporter of "sex outside the lines."

Philosophical differences aside, if your marriage is truly over, it's better for you to work on establishing or reestablishing your identity apart from your mate and building a new life as you rebuild your self-esteem.

Believe this: The pain is finite and a new beginning is possible. Your work will include deep and complete grieving and finding forgiveness for the betrayal. As we write this, we're aware it sounds very cut-and-dried, but we do understand that this will be one of the hardest seasons of your life. We also know you will survive and emerge stronger.

THE FIVE STAGES OF GRIEF

We've found that the grief that follows the death of a relationship is very similar to the stages of grief following the death of a loved one. Understanding the journey of grief will help you to understand that your feelings, while devastating, are normal. Remember, these stages merely represent a typical path and not a prescription for "how to grieve" that you must follow. Grieving is a personal process with no time limit, no one "right" way to do it. Take your time. It is very important to have a support network of people who care about you and will be patient with you as you work through your grief. A good counselor can be essential to this process.

1. Denial

Your first reaction may well be to deny the reality of the situation. This is a normal reaction to overwhelming negative emotions. Denial helps to buffer the immediate shock. This is a temporary response that carries us through the first wave of pain. Then reality hits.

2. Anger

As the masking effects of denial begin to weaken, reality and its pain reemerge. The pain is often deflected from our vulnerable core and is expressed instead as anger, sometimes even rage.

3. Bargaining

Now "if only" becomes our refrain. If only I had done things differently, if only I had seen the signs and put up a roadblock before my mate strayed, if only I were younger, thinner, prettier . . . This is a normal reaction to feelings of helplessness and vulnerability. Even though it hurts to blame ourselves, we do it because we want to feel as if we had some control over the situation, even though we really didn't. Now, our behavior toward our spouse can certainly contribute to the feelings of alienation that lead him or her to stray, but at the end of the day, it's his or her choice whether or not to cheat.

4. Depression

Two types of depression are associated with grief. The first one is a reaction to the practical implications of the loss. It's almost impossible not to worry about finances, the children, the logistics of life. The second type of depression is more subtle and perhaps more private. It is our quiet preparation to separate and to say goodbye. Talking to a counselor may be very helpful.

5. **Acceptance**

This is not a period of happiness, but it must be distinguished from depression. During this phase, the future begins to look brighter, albeit slowly and only a little bit at a time.

THE CONTRACT

The destruction of a relationship often leaves us feeling lost and confused. Not only are we confused about how to live our lives without our significant other, but we are often confused about who we are; we lose touch with our core sense of self. This next exercise will inspire you to navigate the process of rediscovering who you are separate and apart from your life circumstances by taking a trip back to a time when you were just launching into adulthood.

Memory Lane

You are going to take a trip down memory lane. Think about the dreams you had while growing up. Read through this story slowly and deliberately and take plenty of breaks to close your eyes and remember.

I want you to imagine that you are going back in time, back to your teen years, when you were carefree and full of dreams. Think about the first car you ever drove. Whether it was new and shiny or old and broken-down, to you it was an awesome machine. In that car, you experienced your first taste of freedom as you drove around with the windows down and your favorite music playing.

Imagine you are driving in that car and your favorite song comes on. You reach down to turn the volume up. What was the song? Take a moment to remember.

You're happily singing along and you are dreaming of being an adult and making your own decisions. I want you to imagine pulling your car off the road at your favorite spot. It may have been a park near your house or a wooded area, perhaps a spot off a mountain road. You drive your car to your favorite spot and park. Then you step out of your car, climb onto the hood, lie back, and look up at the stars.

Take a moment to consider each of these questions slowly:

- What were your dreams?
- What goals did you have for your life?
- Did you see a bright future ahead of you?
- Were you carefree and able to love?
- What was different about you then?
- What dream have you never shared with anyone?
- Does that dream still exist?

Imagine you are looking up into the night sky and find the brightest star. Ask to be shown your future. Suddenly, the star appears to grow brighter and brighter and you can't seem to pull your eyes away from it. A being appears from within the light and begins floating toward you. You feel no fear as the being comes closer and hovers in the air over you. The being speaks to you. "We have heard your request and I am here to take you to see your future. Just take my hand." You stretch out your arm, and as soon as you touch the being, you begin floating in the air. You are calm and relaxed and eager to see how all of your dreams have turned out.

As you rise higher and higher, you can see the earth below you, spinning. As it slows, you can see your car, now so old it can no longer be driven. You see friends and family and they are much older. You see your old house, which is much smaller than you remembered. The being stops for a moment, and you see yourself at an age when your dreams started to take shape. As you move through the years, you see the stories of your life occur like you are watching a movie.

As you continue on your journey, you see yourself hovering over a building. The being descends with you through the ceiling, and you now see yourself sitting in this very room. The younger version of you is hovering over your head and is now fully aware of your life's journey up to the age you are right now. Ask yourself the following questions:

- Did you think that you would look like you do?
- Are you where you thought you'd be financially? Spiritually? Emotionally? Do your relationships look like you thought they would look?
- Is your younger counterpart excited about what he or she is seeing or saddened by it?
- Did you accomplish your goals, or did you underachieve?
- As you look at your life now, based on your early dreams, would you consider your life a success or a failure?
- Have you become less trusting? Less loving? Less lovable? Have you put up walls? Are you the person you hoped you'd become?
- How have you lost your early vision for life?

Somewhere along the road of life, things happen. We take a few wrong turns or tragedy strikes and we get off track. We're like a car that has hit a pothole and is now out of alignment but still needs to keep moving. The loss of a relationship can cause us to lose our sense of who we are. We feel discarded, worthless, and rejected. These feelings dominate our identity and create terrible imbalance and delusion, and it's time to heal. We are much more than our circumstances, and this needs to be affirmed in our thought life. This exercise is meant to realign your chassis and rediscover parts of yourself that you may have forgotten. Take a look at this list of descriptors and write down any that apply to you:

Acceptable	Joyful
Beautiful	Kind
Capable	Lovable
Caring	Loving
Compassionate	Open
Complete	Pure
Confident	Respectable
Courageous	Strong
Deserving	Trusting
Forgiving	Vulnerable
Forgiven	Warm
Free	Whole
Gentle	Winner
Giving	Worthwhile
Good	Worthy
Honest	

We see the proverb "As a man thinks, so is he" played out every day. It's time to make that work *for* you instead of against you. The destruction of a relationship can turn your thoughts against you, and you may have been listening to your inner critic for too long. If you are thinking critical thoughts about yourself, you are at risk of *becoming* those thoughts. The list of accusations can get embedded in your subconscious and you don't even realize that a recording is playing in your head. It says something like "You are worthless; you don't deserve love. If anyone knew the real you, they would hate you." Research has shown that you actually rewire your brain by your thought life; let's rewire it for our greatest good. In this exercise you will be creating your own personal, truthful affirmation statement of your best you.

Take your list of descriptors and create an affirmation that describes the real you. This will be your personal statement of identity. It represents who you are *now* and includes all of your growth and aspirations. It is a contract, an agreement with yourself on how you will see yourself from now on. It should read something like:

- I am a beautiful, competent, worthy soul.
- I am powerful and good and the architect of my life.
- I am leaving my past in the past because I am free to move forward.
- I am a forgiver at peace with life.

Take your "contract" and commit it to memory. Meditate on it, keep it in a place that you can reference often, put this recording on replay in your mind, and allow this truth to be what takes you from *thinking* to *being*.

KEY TAKEAWAYS FOR THIS CHAPTER

- After infidelity, both partners have to want to fix the marriage in order for it to be successfully repaired.
- Spouses who have been cheated on need time to grieve, and the cheater must be prepared to deal with the blowback resulting from his or her actions.
- If you've been cheated on, you need to focus on healing yourself and rebuilding your own self-esteem.
- You can change your life and your brain by changing your mental tapes. Take a trip down memory lane and remember who you truly are, affirm the best of who you are, create a personal "contract" with yourself, and start now to have the life you've always wanted.

FIGHTING

QUICK QUIZ

When you fight, how do you fight? Can you focus on one thing at a time? Do you save up everything that has made you angry for weeks and let it all out at once in a huge explosion? Do you dig in your heels and passionately argue your position, determined not to let anyone roll over you? Do you hate to fight and shy away when your mate starts an argument because you'd rather do *anything* than have a big conflict? Is fighting your worst nightmare?

Every chapter in this book deals with conflict. All couples fight; of this you can be sure. The question is, how do you deal with conflict in a way that gives you the kind of outcome that you desire? This chapter is all about giving you a winning strategy to fight the good fight and come out of your conflict stronger and closer than when you started.

Justin and Tracy's Story

Justin and his fiancée, Tracy, have been together for five years and recently got engaged. The first thing he did after they became engaged was to move into her apartment. Tracy encouraged him to get rid of a lot of his stuff—old trophies, books, even his beloved poker table—because there wasn't room for all of it. Now Justin is unhappy and says, "I feel like I'm losing my identity."

Their families and friends advised them to compromise, to negotiate who gets to keep what and what has to be thrown out—as if Justin and Tracy hadn't already tried that! This may seem like a straightforward conflict that calls for simple compromise, but as is so often the case, Justin and Tracy couldn't agree because there was something going on beneath this issue. Otherwise, they would have already figured this out and wouldn't have felt the need to bring their problems to Marriage Boot Camp.

When we talked to them, several questions immediately came to mind. Is John's identity truly tied so closely to his "stuff" that getting rid of it would cause him to lose it? That's a red flag. Is his fiancée so controlling that he can't assert what he wants in the relationship? That's also a red flag. Is John fearful of asserting his needs? Is he a doormat? Is he a member of Future Hoarders of America? We needed to help Justin and Tracy uncover the real issue beneath this fight about John's "stuff."

At Marriage Boot Camp we have found that there are several things that become barriers to having a really good fight. Our list includes: competition, past issues that rear their ugly heads in your present conflict, a lack of rules to guide your conflict, and finally, not having a good, solid conflict-resolution process to get from beginning to end with a win-win outcome.

COMPETITION

Two people who have blended their lives together will have conflict—about money, chores, children, time, and a million other little things unique to them as a couple—and it's important to have a healthy way to let out the anger and frustration and work toward a resolution that both partners can live with.

Disagreement can be healthy when it's expressed openly, honestly and without malice. Used as a weapon, when conflict becomes a competition, it tears at the very foundation of a relationship. Especially when one half of the couple is a particularly gifted wordsmith with a sharp tongue. Ask yourself the following questions and take a moment to really think through your response.

- When you fight with your mate, what do you want to achieve from winning the argument?
- How would it make you feel to win?
- Is winning the fight satisfying?
- Does it end the fight?

BOOT CAMP CALL TO ACTION—WITH YOUR MATE

Before we get into the really tough work of learning how to manage conflict, let's have some fun. These exercises from Marriage Boot Camp demonstrate, in a concrete, physical way, the push-pull nature of a fight. Do not do these drills if you're angry with each other; pick a time when you're both open to having fun and learning something. Because these are physical exercises, be extremely gentle and careful not to hurt each other; that is certainly not the goal or the point. Do not read the results until you have completed both drills.

Spot War

For this game, grab your partner and a timer (the timer on your cell phone will work just fine). Stand face-to-face, then take two small steps to your left, away from each other, so that you are an arm's length apart. Reach out and clasp your right hands.

The objective is to keep your partner from pulling you off your spot while at the same time keeping your own feet from moving.

Do not hurt anyone. If one of you moves your feet off your spot, you lose. If both of you move your feet, both of you lose. Set the timer for twenty seconds and have at it! Then STOP!

Now, before we analyze the spot war, let's go ahead and try this next drill.

Tug-of-War

Every good Boot Camp has a tug-of-war, right? Stand facing each other, each holding the end of a towel. Be sure that there is enough distance between you to keep the towel taut. Now imagine a mark on the floor equidistant between the two of you. The object of the game is to get your mate's end of the towel over onto your side of the dividing line. You cannot move your feet. You have twenty seconds. Go!

Spot and Tug-of-War Results

Who won the spot war? Who won the tug-of-war? If you think one of you won, then you are both losers!

The object of the spot war was to keep your feet from being moved off your spot. If you both had just stood still, neither one of you would've been moved off your spot, and you both would've won. In the tug-of-war, remember that the object was to get your mate's side of the towel onto your side of the dividing line. Well, if you had simply flipped the towel around, so that your side was now on your mate's side and vice versa, then you both would have won.

What can you learn from this? We are all taught to be competitive, and some of us are determined to win at all costs. The problem is that although we joke about life being a "game," a relationship is not a game. When there's one winner and one loser in a relationship dispute, the relationship itself loses. Win-win is the only healthy option. If you find yourself in a win-lose situation, then you both lose.

Candy and Henry's Story

Candy is one smart lady, and Henry loves this about her. So why is Henry mad at Candy? They were talking about a tax policy issue and Candy was able to show Henry that his position, while well meaning, was wrong. But instead of Henry appreciating being schooled, he was irritated. This is a classic example of how win-lose ends up being lose-lose. A fight erupted, with Henry telling Candy that she always had to be right and Candy telling Henry that he was a sore loser.

When you get competitive in a relationship, you always lose. If you hurt your spouse, you always lose. Have you ever won a fight with a loved one without causing some kind of damage? Of course not. Despite your best apologies, words cannot be unspoken.

Let's try another drill to demonstrate our point.

Arm Wrestling

Get into an arm-wrestling stance with your mate. The object of this game is to see how many times you can pin each other's arm to the table.

Ready, set, and go.

The way that you win the arm-wrestling match of marriage is to allow your mate to pull your arm over to his side, and vice versa. With a soft arm and a giving heart, the two of you can go back and forth many, many times, which is exactly the point. Two people who can gently influence each other in a back-and-forth dance, without competition, are living in a happy marriage.

Tammy and Ron's Story

Tammy and Ron were two avid marathoners who loved sports and loved the thrill of competition. In fact, it was the thrill of competing in athletics that drew them together in the first place. After being paired up in a couples tennis match against the club champions and soundly beating them, well, they fell in love, got married, and blended their two same-age daughters into one big, happy family. Then the first Christmas was upon them and, as tradition would have it, Ron and his daughter, Mindy, sat down and made a wish list of gifts and goodies that Mindy was dreaming of. Tammy's daughter, Jordan, got wind of this, went to her mom, and presented her wish list. Tammy was shocked! This was beyond anything that they had ever bought in Christmases past, but Jordan assured her that it was the new normal according to Ron. Not to be outdone, Tammy said fine and added a few more goodies to the list, which now started to put a strain on the budget, and the marriage. After several volleys of passive-aggressiveness, they reached an impasse and called us, saying they were fighting over money. Both of them had sound logic for their point of view. They used phrases like "We have to be fair" and "We don't

want one girl to feel favored over the other," but the truth was
that they both *needed* to win and were prepared to go bank-
rupt in the process. They also had let the kids come between
them. The girls were no dummies and knew how to push the
right button to get what they wanted. Well, in true Boot Camp
style we challenged them to a competition of spot war, tug-of-
war, and arm wrestling. The point was clear—they would do
anything to win. Then Jim and Elizabeth showed them how
the games *could* be played to have a win-win solution. The
good news is that a lightbulb went on, showing them that winning worked on the court but wasn't working in their relationship. At this point we were able to teach them the Marriage
Boot Camp conflict-resolution process that you will find at
the end of this chapter, and they were finally able to resolve
this conflict, save their savings, and create a stronger connection.

HOT BUTTONS

Now that we've covered how competition can destroy your relationship, let us ask another question. Do you sometimes find yourself overreacting to something your spouse does or says and later
wondering what the heck you were thinking? Do you have pet
peeves, things guaranteed to get under your skin? Pet peeves,
whether dirty dishes left in the sink or a spouse who always has to
have the last word, can actually be symptoms of a childhood
wound. The key is to pay attention to times when you overreact
and let this lead you to the original wound. At Marriage Boot
Camp we call these old wounds "hot buttons."

Allison and Mike's Story

Allison has a big personality and a stressful high-profile job that sometimes causes her to come home from work in a really bad mood. As the business owner, she can't call out a client or vent to her employees about problems with annoying clients or staff. The only person she can share all the nitty-gritty details with (and trust not to repeat them) is her husband, Mike.

Mike's job gave him flexible hours and the ability to work from home, which, given Allison's job, was the only reason either one of them ever had any clean laundry. Allison acknowledged how much Mike did to keep almost everything in their life running smoothly and tried to remember to demonstrate appreciation for his efforts, but she admitted that she tended to be critical of the way he did things when she was feeling overwrought because of work.

Mike had a much more mellow personality than his wife, and he was truly doing his very best to be the support system that Allison needed at home. But Mike had had it and was tired of Allison coming home and exploding on him for no apparent reason, yelling at him about his failings. It was slowly destroying their marriage.

Mike understood intellectually that Allison's moods had to do with work and that her criticisms weren't really about him, but he felt the abuse was simply too much to bear. He didn't understand (because men's brains work differently from women's) how some problem with an employee or a client could end up being a big fight about how he hadn't taken care of mowing the lawn or giving the dog a bath like he'd promised. Allison was mean and nasty during these bouts, even throwing the word "divorce" around, though the arguments were usually about something completely manageable. Mike was afraid that one day he would just have to leave, but because he loved her, he didn't want to give up.

Allison admitted everything he said and was ashamed. She tried not to take her work frustrations out on Mike but sometimes wasn't able to control her mouth.

At least Allison had the good sense to understand that her reactions didn't match the situation and were toxic to their relationship. Allison's overreaction to Mike's housekeeping "failings" signaled a hidden wound, a hot button. With Allison, we had some digging to do.

Elizabeth's Story

When I was six or seven years old, there was a certain group of boys who would taunt me and call me the N-word because of my dark skin. One day they pushed me down on the playground, and I hit my head. I woke up to find myself in bed and learned that I had a concussion from the fall. Without being aware, I developed a negative self-image from this and believed that I was inferior because of my skin color and my mixed race. Over time this morphed into an adult "hot button," and I became extremely sensitive to criticism of any kind.

We all have hot buttons. Hot buttons generally develop early in life, at a time when we simply don't have the ability to make sense of some of our own suffering. They remain with us and stay in an immature, primitive state unless they get flushed to the surface and into our awareness. Imagine what this underground time bomb can do to our relationships! Yes, they can cause us to do and say stupid things that leave scars.

Mario's Story

Mario was born to a single mother, and while his father lived in the same town, he never came to see Mario. Life was very hard because his mother had to work two jobs for them to survive, and she left Mario home alone a lot. He fantasized about his father coming to claim him and create a whole new life for him, but mostly he wanted to have his worth validated by this phantom father. As Mario grew in years, his longing turned into anger. He recalls one Christmas when he was thirteen years old. He had earned enough money shoveling snow to buy his father, a father he had seen but never met, a Christmas snow globe. He remembers walking in the cold and knocking on the door of the house where he thought his father lived. The woman his father lived with answered the door and called for him, knowing that this boy was his son. He heard his father yell from inside the house, "Tell him I'm not home." The door closed, and Mario stood there for a moment, held the snow globe in his fist, and punched it through the glass in the door. He then walked home with a bleeding hand, vowing never to let anybody get to him like that again. Well, the vow didn't work. That wound of rejection would get poked, and Mario would feel like punching a fist through a glass door again. Rejection was Mario's hot button.

Mario is now married, and he and his wife sought help at the Marriage Boot Camp because he would explode with a vicious, explosive temper whenever his rejection hot button was poked. Mario would then come down from his triggered state and hate himself for the damage he was causing. Clearly, powerful rejection by his father had left the wound that was now Mario's hot button, and this would show up in his marriage. When Mario's wife hit his hot button, Mario could feel all of the primitive pain that his father's past rejection created and he would lash out. The key to resolving this dysfunctional pattern was not telling Mario that he needed to control his temper; he already knew that. We needed to first go back and to get at the root of this behavior, this hot button.

BOOT CAMP CALL TO ACTION

Take a moment and read through this list of common things that push our buttons.

I GET MY HOT BUTTONS PUSHED:
- when I feel criticized or compared.
- when I feel made fun of, humiliated.
- when I feel inadequate or stupid.
- when I feel unappreciated, ignored.
- when I feel taken advantage of, powerless.
- when I feel unfairly accused, distrusted.
- when I feel disrespected.
- when I feel unloved.

Do any of these resonate for you? Can you think of others? Close your eyes for a moment and really feel the pain of your hot buttons. Being as specific as you can, make a list of your hot buttons in your journal or notebook.

Allison and Mike's Story Continued

After Allison and Mike came to the Marriage Boot Camp and went through the exercise of identifying hot buttons, a light-bulb went on for both of them. In Allison's case, having to stuff her feelings with clients and employees made her crazy. She then would go home and lay it on Mike, with Mike getting the point of the dagger at times. The feelings for Allison were very real, but the source of the feelings was blurry. Unidentified inner feelings often get projected outward, free radicals seeking a place to land, usually on the person closest to us, in this case Mike. What Allison discovered was that many of these angry feelings actually came from her relationship with her abusive father. As far back as she could remember, she'd never talked back to him, no matter what he said or did to her; he simply would not allow her to express her anger or dissatisfaction, so she buried it down deep inside, white-knuckling through the emotion. She did not learn how to express her feelings or emotions in a healthy way as a child because it simply wasn't permitted. Well, now she's a grown woman and these feelings will not stay stuffed.

Now Allison realizes that when she fights with Mike over truly small things, the rage she feels inside is very real, but she's overreacting. It appears that something small can trigger those feelings of having to stuff her righteous indignation and then, boom, she goes off.

Now that Allison understands that some of her overreactions can be tied to this early wounding, she has a better chance of getting control over them so that she doesn't punish the people she loves for the things that a past abuser did.

Engaging Your Mate

Throughout the book, we've been talking about the patterns of our lives, from our ABCs to our hot buttons. Now we're going to take a deeper dive to try to root out the history of your hot buttons so they won't muddy the water and show up in your conflict. Why are they what they are? What created them?

MARRIAGE BOOT CAMP QUICK SCRIPT

Give your mate a quick explanation of what a hot button is and take some time to share from your heart about your past. Say something like:

"I just read an interesting topic in the *Marriage Boot Camp* book about 'hot buttons.' It really helped me understand myself better and made me realize that I may be hurting you with them, which is the last thing I want to do to someone I love so much. A hot button is an old wound from the past, probably from childhood, that gets stirred up in our present and makes us do things that we later regret. I'd like to share some things about myself that I discovered, and I'd also love to hear about things that might be hot buttons for you."

Take out your list of hot buttons and ask your partner to make one of his own. Read the "I Get My Hot Buttons Pushed When" section to your mate to help him make his list of things that resonate with him. Then, beside every button, both of you write down the historical origin of your button. If you think the hot button got its start in your current relationship, please dig deeper and look for the real roots.

Take turns sharing your stories, telling each other what your hot buttons are and how they got their start.

Once you've gone through your list, exchange lists and mirror back each of your mate's hot buttons. This time, take turns telling each other, or mirroring, what you just learned about your partner's hot buttons. Your mirror will sound something like this: "You get your button pushed when I disagree with you. It makes you feel put down, and it takes you back to your dad telling you that you were stupid and didn't know crap." Try to spend at least one minute talking to each other about each particular hot button. Be aware that this exercise will likely lead to much longer and deeper conversations about hot buttons later on. That's a good thing. Understanding what makes you and your mate tick will give you empathy for each other and is key to having a long, healthy, and happy marriage.

Elizabeth's Story

Remember the story about the new car Jim bought me right after we got married? That pushed my hot button, and I was angry and about to blow, a state that we call being "triggered." We hadn't been together long enough to know each other's hot buttons at that point, and I'm surprised Jim didn't look at me as though I were completely crazy, but the truth was that I felt disrespected by the gesture. I responded viscerally, not taking the time to process my feelings, and as a result I said things I wish I hadn't to my brand-new husband, whom I dearly loved and who had just given me a wonderful gift. From Jim's perspective, I had dismissed his method of communicating his love for me (something we talked about in chapter one).

MARRIAGE BOOT CAMP "3RS"

We don't want you to open up any old wounds before you have the tools to handle them. We've found that simply being aware of our hot buttons and what caused them can lessen our overreaction. But at some point you're going to get a hot button pushed and you will be triggered, so we developed a tool called the "3Rs." It stands for "recognize," "relax," and "reassure."

R—Recognize

Awareness is always first. The thing you need to do when you get a hot button pushed is to *recognize* it and understand that's why you're feeling agitated, angry, frustrated, or about to do something stupid. When this happens, you need to recognize your feelings and say, "I'm feeling triggered."

R—Relax

In order to break the chain reaction of conflict, you must change your physical state. When you get angry, a biological process takes place in your body that fuels the fight-or-flight reaction. Your body is flooded with adrenaline and noradrenaline as well as a cocktail of other neurotransmitters that fire you up. It is very useful if you are running from a mammoth or preparing to beat up the beast, but it's terrible when you're having an argument with your mate. We learned from the Navy SEALs a breathing technique that flushes these chemicals out of your system, and it takes only twenty seconds. It's called square breathing or 4x4 breathing and it looks like this: Breathe in for a count of four, hold your breath for another count of four, breathe out for a count of four, and then hold your empty lungs for another count of four. At the Marriage Boot Camp seminar, we have the participants put their hands out in front of them, touch their middle finger to their thumb, and say, "Ommmmm." This gets a good laugh, but it teaches an important lesson. Change your physical state as soon as you recognize that you are being triggered. It will slow down the speeding train just long enough to allow you to change course.

R—Reassure

Finally, you must reassure yourself. The way you talk to yourself is very powerful and can even be life-defining. Say to yourself, "I can handle this. I am safe and loved." Visualize giving yourself a hug or even wrap your arms around yourself as you repeat, "I can handle this."

Practice makes perfect. The 3Rs, if practiced, will eventually become second nature, and the entire 3R process will happen in less than a second. It's as simple as saying "I'm feeling triggered" while taking a deep breath and reassuring yourself with an affirming thought.

BOOT CAMP CALL TO ACTION

Push My Button

In the Marriage Boot Camp seminar we do a drill called "Push My Button." Since our seminar is a controlled environment, we are able to do this safely and no one gets hurt. You can do this at home, but be warned, you will feel triggered. If you are at risk for getting triggered and physically acting out, we suggest you simply imagine walking through these steps as a visualization.

The purpose of this drill is to practice the 3Rs and not overreact when your buttons are pushed. You want to really feel the emotion but not react.

Stand up and face each other.

The first "pusher" up at bat will put both of his hands on his partner's shoulders, give a gentle push, and use a phrase that pushes his partner's hot button. Pushees, you will let your mate push you backward for a full step, and remember, *do not react*. You will be getting a physical push along with an emotional push. The pusher will physically (but gently) push three times, saying the hot-button phrase each time. Then you switch and repeat the process. At the end you both should be feeling pretty fired up.

Now we combine the push with the 3Rs. One of you will push while the other practices his response; it will be a push-respond pattern as follows:

- Push—*recognize*. "I'm getting triggered."
- Push—*relax*. Take a deep breath.

■ Push—*reassure*. Give yourself a hug and say, "I can handle this."

The key to managing your hot buttons is learning to control them as opposed to letting them control you. Practice makes perfect; if you practice the 3Rs over and over, you will find that they become second nature.

TRIGGER TALK

Let me add one last variation to the hot-buttons discussion. First, let us make a distinction between trigger talk and being triggered. Being triggered is an internal state that needs to be recognized before you act out and do something stupid. Trigger talk is the "something stupid." You get triggered and then the junk starts flying out of your mouth. How many of you have ever said or been told something like:

■ I never loved you.
■ I hate you.
■ I wish I'd never married you.
■ You'll never amount to anything.

We call this trigger talk. This is the stupid stuff we say when we get angry. It's always emotional language as opposed to logical language, but this trigger talk can get stuck in your mate's logic box and turn into bitterness that can destroy a marriage. So, what do we do when this type of verbal abuse occurs? That's right, we recognize that an emotional language is being spoken and we respond with emotional language combined with truth and logic so that we can de-escalate the situation. For example, if I am the perpetrator, I need to use my 3Rs, and when I am calm I might say: "I'm so sorry. When I said that, it was not true or logical. I blurted that out emotionally in the heat of the moment and I would take it back if I could. Please forgive me." If I am the victim, I might say (right after the 3Rs): "Wow, that really hurt. I know that you don't mean what you just said, but I have to tell you that even though it doesn't make sense, it still hurts."

Scott and Jeani's Story

When Scott was growing up, his dad used to tell him that he was lazy and that's why he didn't achieve at the level of his brilliant older sister. Over and over this got branded into his brain: "Scott, you're just lazy!" Scott had two choices: He could identify with the message or he could reject the message. He chose to reject this harsh judgment and took an "I'll show you!" attitude. This worked very well for him, as he became extremely successful and quite wealthy. But there remained a fly in the ointment. When his wife, Jeani, sometimes asked him, in *just that way*, "What have you been doing all day?" it would send his mind back to his father and he would react in the same way that he did then: turn his back and walk away. That worked really well in his relationship with his father, but not so much with his wife. She felt ignored and disrespected—and the fight was on.

We helped Scott do an archaeological dig into his own psyche, and he found the little nugget buried there from his father. Luckily, we had some tools for him to handle his old wounds.

BOOT CAMP CALL TO ACTION—WITH YOUR MATE

Take a moment to think about any trigger talk that you have stuck in your craw and ask your mate to do the same. Journaling about it in a notebook can be very helpful in finding the root cause. This can be a deeply emotional exercise, and you and your mate may want some help with this. When you dig up old wounds, it's like scratching off a scab and you run the risk of being rewounded and then triggered. We recommend sharing your story with a trusted friend, a support group, or a counselor, and not just once. You may need to tell your story over and over to take enough of the sting out of it before you share it with your mate. Once your narrative is clear, you will need to be validated by the person closest to you, your mate, but don't make the mistake of thinking that he or she has finely tuned therapeutic skills. Let us teach you the important skill of validation.

VALIDATE YOUR MATE

Validating, like mirroring, is a very important tool. When you validate your mate, you're saying, "I understand why you feel the way you feel, and it makes sense to me; you are not crazy." You don't necessarily have to feel the same, or even agree with your partner, but you must empathize and respect his or her feelings. This is a high-level skill because sometimes it feels like the frustration being communicated is aimed at you, and frankly, sometimes it is. The question is, do you want to remain connected to your mate despite the storms of life? If your answer is yes, I want my relationship to work, then it does absolutely no good to defend or argue in heated moments. Validation will de-escalate the emotion so that you can get to the place of having a good, productive fight.

Here are a few examples:

"It makes me furious when I come home to a filthy house!" Validate by saying, "I get it. When the house is a mess, it drives you crazy. I understand why you would feel that way." Then *stop*! Resist the temptation to add the "but . . ."

"My boss is a jerk!" Validate by saying, "I totally understand! He would drive me crazy if I had to work with him!"

"Why am I always waiting for you? Can't you be on time?" Validate by saying, "I hear your frustration and I know that having to wait drives you crazy."

Don't take the bait. Continue to validate until the fever gets out of the conversation. Once the energy is de-escalated, then you can have a problem-solving session, but not before. You'll end up creating additional offenses on top of the initial offense. Then you'll have a yarn ball of junk that becomes impossible to unravel.

Scott and Jeani's Story Continued

Jeani was better able to understand why Scott would snap at her and walk away in light of the trigger talk that lived rent-free in Scott's head. Because of her love for him and her desire to help, she listened to Scott share his story and saw how it affected their marriage. She was able to empathize with how his father's voice was at work when Scott would walk away from her after saying, "I'm hard at work. What do you think I'm doing?" Instead of accusing Scott of being rude (which he was), Jeanie was now able to say, "I understand how you feel, and it makes perfect sense in light of your story." This diminished the pain, and Scott was able to own his trigger and step up with an apology for being rude. Both of them came to understand the power of validation.

WHEN YOU REACH THE POINT OF NO RETURN

Have you ever had your hot buttons pushed to the point of no return? You get so hurt or angry that you just lose control or totally shut down? What happens next? That's right, the discussion goes nowhere. Make no mistake—you will *not* be able to continue to problem solve. All action must stop, and you both must back off!

This has to be a hard-and-fast rule: When one person declares, "I need a time-out," it is both parties' responsibility to back off. Take fifteen minutes out of the ring to cool off.

Be sure to check in after fifteen minutes; if you need more time, tell your mate and take it. However, do *not* turn this tool into a weapon! Avoiders may try to put themselves in time-out just to stop the argument. That isn't going to work if your desire is to resolve conflict. You have to hang in there to the end. So don't waste time and prolong the argument by taking unnecessary breaks to avoid the inevitable.

NOTE: If one of you gets triggered to the point of being violent or dangerous, stop the discussion immediately and GET HELP! If you think things are getting too rough or turning in a bad direction, cease talking and get out of there. If you cannot leave, call a friend for assistance. If necessary, call 911. Conflict resolution will bring up serious emotional responses in you and your mate, but these emotional responses should never translate in any way into physical violence.

In summary, understanding your hot buttons is part of the bigger picture of knowing yourself and having the clarity and discipline to move toward your mate instead of away from your mate when conflict arises. Knowing yourself and having the tools to manage your emotions, your triggers, and your hot buttons will go a long way toward success in the arena of conflict resolution in your relationship. So let's jump right into the arena.

CONFLICT RESOLUTION

RULES OF ENGAGEMENT

Before we enter the arena of conflict resolution, we want to make sure that you and your mate have some solid rules of engagement. Many people neglect to establish rules about how to fight. Remember, if you fail to plan, you plan to fail. The "Rules of Engagement" of Marriage Boot Camp will help you manage conflict and keep your fights productive.

1. **Same Team**

    Know that you are both on the same team, fighting for your relationship, not to make a point, not to win, not to beat your mate down. Attack the issue, not each other. It may be helpful to remember and for each of you to periodically say out loud, "You are not my enemy."

2. One Play

You can only handle one issue at a time! Stay on topic and don't allow the conversation to snowball! A rolling snowball picks up all the garbage in its path and gets bigger and bigger and becomes impossible to stop! Don't bring up past arguments or other unresolved issues. This requires discipline, but know that if you break this rule, the odds of you reaching a good solution are virtually nonexistent. This rule is particularly difficult for spewers, whose idea of a good argument is to bring up everything their mate has ever done wrong in the history of the relationship.

3. Stay in the Game

Coaches often teach their players to "play hurt," meaning that even if you get bumped and bruised, push past the pain and stay focused on the goal. If you are an avoider and you tend to run out on your team, your relationships will suffer. Take one for the team and stay in the fight! If your spouse needs to have an argument to resolve a new or ongoing conflict, do not avoid it. Suck it up and face it head-on so you can move past it together.

4. LUV: Listen-Understand-Validate

This concept goes all the way back to the very roots of psychotherapy and has worked for decades. During a conflict:

Listen. Stop, pay attention, and really focus on what your partner is saying. You must put your own opinions, feelings, and logic on hold for the moment.

Understand. Try to understand things from your mate's point of view and let them know that you get it. This is an intellectual process of verbalizing another's point of view with the powerful communication skill called mirroring. When your mate is done sharing, "mirror" back what your mate said with "What I heard you say is . . ."

Validate. In addition to intellectually understanding your mate's point of view, you must validate that point of view from an emotional perspective. This does not mean you must agree. Validation is an exercise in empathy. Empathy is not sympathy or feeling sorry for your mate. In validating your mate, you must use your heart to truly understand your mate's position *emotionally.* You can say, "I see why you would think that; that makes sense to me . . ." Use your imagination to really feel it. Show that you recognize his or her feelings with language such as "I see that you're scared" or "I know you're frustrated."

5. No Personal Fouls

If you're a sports fan, you know the impact that a personal foul can have on your game. In the game of managing conflict, here is our list of bad plays that should be avoided at all costs:

- Name calling
- Cursing
- Button pushing
- Third-party testimonials (my sister thinks so too!)
- Superlatives (you *never*, you *always*)
- Nonverbal responses (eye rolling, head shaking, sighing, etc.)
- Threats

6. Time-out

Have you ever gotten overheated and said or done something that you wish you hadn't? Remember "Trigger Talk"? When this happens, you need to *back off*. Stop the argument and take a time-out. Conflict avoiders may not use this rule as a weapon to avoid finishing the fight. Agree to get back in the game and finish the disagreement as soon as possible. This is very important! The time-out can be very difficult on the pursuing mate, but if you have a time limit on how long you will be gone, it will take the anxiety out of the break. Pursuers can take a moment to check social media, get something to drink, or go to the bathroom and relax. Take a fifteen-minute break, then check back in to see if you can continue in a productive way.

7. Score

Strive for win-win solutions that benefit everybody. The key to a win-win is ending up closer and more connected than before the discussion. As we discovered in the tug-of-war, in marriage "win-lose" is really "lose-lose," because if your mate is unhappy, you will be unhappy, too. Nobody wins in a power struggle! Remember "Needs and Wants" or "Love Dots"? You should know by now how to fill your mate's Love Account. Negotiate and barter if need be to find a compromise that works for both of you. Maybe she agrees to do all the shopping if he'll help put everything away from those monster runs to Costco, or he does the laundry, which she wants, and in return, she gives him more sex, which he wants. Does this mean you're trading tasks for sex? Heck yeah! If it brings peace and closeness, that is win-win! Be creative! Whatever works for you both as a couple is win-win. Get to a win-win solution, whatever it takes.

8. Spike the Ball!

Excessive celebration is highly encouraged! When you get through a tough conflict, make sure that you celebrate together. High five! Don't just put it behind you; acknowledge that you've had a success in your relationship. Go out for ice cream, have a happy hour, or—everyone's favorite—have makeup sex! Mark this moment by spending time together in a conflict-free way.

STEP-BY-STEP PROCESS OF CONFLICT RESOLUTION

Now that you understand the ground rules, we're going to give you step-by-step instructions for conflict resolution. We have used this method both in the Marriage Boot Camp seminars and on TV. One memorable couple told us that they'd been fighting about one issue for six years and by using the step-by-step process were able to resolve it for the first time. These steps will work with your mate, your kids, and even your colleagues, and it is astonishingly effective (unless, of course, you're the guy who complained that his wife came into the bathroom while he was in the bathtub, took out a blow-dryer, turned it on, and held it over the water, threatening to drop it if things didn't go her way. True story, and no, we don't have a tool for that).

Here's the deal. You are both going to have to stop being hard-headed, stubborn, and one-sided. You may never get one hundred percent of what you want, but you can get connection, peace, and harmony in your marriage. You will need to replace your "my way or the highway" attitude with a "what do I need to do to have a happy home" attitude.

Here's the drill. Pick *one issue* that you currently struggle with and take turns giving each other your perspective and your proposed solutions. It is important to go very slowly and methodically so that you avoid having it snowball into a huge disaster. Here is the entire end-to-end process:

1. Focus on one issue only and write down the ABC diagram.
2. Hear each other's perspective and feelings.
3. Mirror back and validate each other's perspective.
4. Hear each side's best-case solution.
5. Hear what each of you would be willing to settle for.
6. Negotiate a mutual resolution.

Now let's take each step one at a time.

STEP 1. Decide on *one* conflict that *both* of you want to resolve. DO NOT TRY TO SOLVE THE ISSUE JUST YET! This will be the "A" in your ABC diagram. Here are some typical issues: money, sex, disciplining the children, friendships outside the marriage, cleaning the house, time management (e.g., electronics, punctuality, family time).

Once you have agreed on one topic to discuss, you're each going to break the issue down into Action-Belief-Consequences (refer to chapter one if you need a refresher on the drill). Separately, write down your own interpretation of the problem in the ABC format. Don't solve it yet. *Just write it down.*

You do not have to agree on the B or the C; in fact, if you did agree, you wouldn't be fighting. Here's an example:

Her perspective: When you (A) challenge me about every penny I spend, I believe (B) that you think I'm irresponsible, and I (C) feel belittled and powerless, which causes a cold war and me to shut down.

His perspective: When you (A) spend money that we don't have, I believe (B) that we are going to be ruined financially, and then (C) I feel terrified and take away the credit cards and a crap storm starts.

STEP 2. Conflict resolution starts with explaining your perspective. This should come from the heart; try to be as real as you can be and speak from a purely selfish point of view. Give your side of the story in as much detail as possible and explain how it makes you feel. Take no more than two minutes to do this.

Your partner's job at this point is to listen carefully and then move on to step three. Make no mistake: It's very challenging to be the listener! You have to put your feelings, thoughts, and opinions on hold for the moment, *even if what you are hearing is making you mad.* This is your time to *listen!* You do not have to agree with what the other person is saying.

STEP 3. Mirror back what was just said: "What I heard you say is . . ." or "I know you feel . . ." This should last no more than thirty seconds.

Now switch it up and have your mate give his or her side of the issue and be sure to mirror back what you heard.

At this point, the only thing the two of you should have done is state the problem from your perspective. You should not be interrupting, challenging your mate's version of events, correcting errors, or defending yourself! You do not have to agree with their version of the story; you simply have to LUV (listen, understand, and validate) your mate by mirroring back what he or she just said. If you are getting triggered, you have just made this about *you* instead of focusing on having a happy home.

Remember, your perspective is your perspective and your mate's perspective is your mate's perspective. You do not have to agree with his version of the story; you simply have to empathize with the dilemma by mirroring back what he said. As we just explained, if you are being triggered by something in his perspective, you have just made this exercise about you rather than about finding a win-win solution.

STEP 4. You have now heard each other's side of the story. You've also heard each other's feelings about this particular issue. Now you will each share your suggested solution. Remember to stay on *one* topic.

Spend one minute telling your mate your best-case solution to the problem and how you'd feel about getting this issue resolved and behind you. Your partner will listen and mirror back what you just said, for one minute. Then switch places; you become the listener while your mate explains his or her best-case solution and how it would feel to have it resolved. Take one minute to mirror back what your mate just said.

STEP 5. Now that you have heard each other's ideas about resolving the issue, it's time for you to compromise and share what you would be willing to settle for in order to resolve the conflict.

Take one minute to describe exactly what you're willing to settle for, which now incorporates some of what you heard about your mate's solution, and then have your mate take thirty seconds to mirror back what he or she heard. Then switch places and repeat.

STEP 6. You should now have as much information as you need to resolve any conflict, provided you are willing to give a little. Negotiate, barter, compromise, or sacrifice. Get creative! The goal is to solve the problem in a manner where you both feel like you are winners and brings you closer.

Take three minutes to negotiate a solution that is a *win-win* for both of you. Once you have agreed on a solution, write it down as a game plan. Be sure to include a commitment to make this work.

Conflict resolution is a complex process that you have to take step-by-step, but if you do, we promise you can successfully resolve the issues that plague your relationships once and for all. You can't skip any of the steps along the way and get the same result. With practice, the process becomes easier and should become the standard by which you resolve conflicts, rather than the exception to the rule.

> Here are the steps for conflict resolution in a
> relationship:
>
> - Focus the conflict on *one* issue with a complete
>   ABC diagram.
> - Hear each side's perspective and feelings.
> - Mirror back the other's perspective and feelings.
> - Hear each side's best-case solution.
> - Hear what each of you would be willing to settle
>   for.
> - Negotiate a mutual resolution.

Now you have a working process for conflict resolution that you can use at home, at work, with friends, with your kids . . . with anybody, really.

KEY TAKEAWAYS FOR THIS CHAPTER

- Win-win solutions are the only option for a happy marriage.
- Hot buttons are wounds from the past that can affect your present conflict.

- You must manage your hot buttons (or they will manage you) by using the 3Rs.
- Trigger talk is a toxic, damaging by-product of a hot button.
- "Rules of Engagement" are the necessary guardrails for a productive fight.
- Conflict resolution is a step-by-step process that everyone should use.

9

WRESTLING WITH THE PAST

QUICK QUIZ

Have you or your mate suffered abuse in the past? Have you experienced trauma or a tragic loss? Do you find that you sabotage your relationship and wonder why? Perhaps there are things in your past that aren't actually in the past but continue to influence your present. The point of this chapter is to identify every roadblock that gets in the way of having a happy, committed, connected marriage, and we have found in the Marriage Boot Camp that having great relational skills is often not enough. Sometimes the baggage from our past stops us dead in our tracks. If that is the case, this chapter will help you gain the tools to manage those things from the past and move forward.

Jamie and Thomas's Story

Jamie and Thomas came to the Marriage Boot Camp saying that they were in constant conflict. Jamie never wants to have sex or withholds sex when she's angry. Thomas has a terrible temper, and when he gets triggered he can become violent. Jamie said all she wanted was for Thomas to be the father to their three children that she and Thomas never had. But without a good role model, Thomas was struggling; he had the best of intentions, but he was stuck in overwhelming feelings of shame and inadequacy.

We realized that Thomas and Jamie both had had tragic childhoods, rife with unresolved wounds that were now largely unconscious. These unconscious wounds remained underground because both Thomas and Jamie kept them there, primarily by remaining disciplined and sometimes superficial. Even though Thomas and Jamie worked very hard to suppress their baggage, it surfaced at times when exhaustion, pain, and stress were at their peak. We knew that Jamie and Thomas had to start digging into their life history with a tool that we call life mapping.

BOOT CAMP CALL TO ACTION

Life Maps

The first step toward ridding ourselves of the baggage of the past is to bring it out into the open. In this exercise, you are going to create a life map that will represent the defining moments of your life, both high and low. We recommend that you get a large foam poster board, but you can use whatever materials you have at your disposal, such as a notebook, sketchbook, or tablet. You will be plotting out your life visually with whatever media you choose.

Your life map will be your unique creation. To help you get started, here are a few examples:

TIMELINE—You might like a simple timeline with significant dates and events shown as they occurred.

LIFE EVENTS

					Graduated College			
		Broken Arm			Job in Advertising	Married		
	Kindergarten		First Boyfriend			Divorced		
Born 7/5/1956				Graduated High School	Job with Levi Strauss	Married		

1950	1955	1960	1965	1970	1975	1980	1985	1990

Skiing Accident

Moved to Indianapolis · Ilsa Born

ROAD MAP—Maybe you see your life as a wandering road, each twist and turn a memory.

GRAPH—Perhaps you see your life as a series of highs and lows illustrated with dates and events as peaks and valleys.

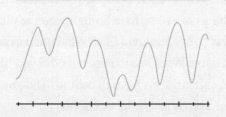

BULLET POINTS—You might choose to record your life as a simple list of dates, names, and events.

- BORN 7/5/1956
- KINDERGARTEN 1961
- BROKEN ARM 1964
- SKIING ACCIDENT 1965
- FIRST BOYFRIEND 1971
- GRADUATED HIGH SCHOOL 1974
- GRADUATED COLLEGE 1978

- MOVED TO INDIANAPOLIS 1978
- JOB IN ADVERTISING 1979
- JOB WITH LEVI STRAUSS 1980
- MARRIED 1986
- DIVORCED 1987
- MARRIED 1989
- ILSA BORN 1989

ARTISTIC—Some people take an abstract approach, illustrating their lives in pictures of people, places, symbols, or events.

Before you get started on the map, take a moment to reflect back across the span of your life and answer these questions in your mind:

- What things or events have hurt you the most?
- What things or events have brought you the most joy?
- What was your childhood like? What good experiences did you have? What bad experiences did you have?
- Did you excel in school or fall behind? Did you graduate from high school or college?

- Have you been able to fulfill your dreams and goals? Did you get that dream job, or lose a job?
- Have you experienced the death of a loved one?
- Have you experienced the birth or the death of a child?
- Have you experienced divorce, either your own or your parents'?
- Have you experienced an injury or major health issue that has held you back in life?

It's your life map—draw it your way. Just pick a memory and start illustrating.

Engaging Your Mate

This is a great project to do with your mate. It's fun and creative as well as enlightening. Once you've completed your life maps, take turns walking each other through them. Use the Marriage Boot Camp first rule of communication: When one person is talking, the other person is listening. To keep this a comfortable and safe space for sharing, make a pact that any information that is shared will not be used against each other.

Take turns describing a high or low point in your life. Then have the other person mirror back what he or she just learned about you.

Finally, share with your mate any events that may still be affecting you today.

DEVELOPMENTAL STAGES OF LIFE

Now that you have your life map drawn, let's consider at what stage of your development your wounding may have taken place. Erik Erikson, a renowned developmental psychologist and psychoanalyst, created one of the best-known personality theories in the world. As discussed in chapter six, Erikson describes psychosocial development as a series of life stages. The question that needs to be addressed now is, what does it look like in adulthood when the attachment needs of the child go unmet?

Stage 1: Attachment

Healthy adult relationships should show an appreciation for interdependence and relatedness. Those who did not get their needs met in the attachment stage of life will have relationships marked by swings between being overly dependent to being detached and independent. An adult who was well cared for in this stage of life can say with confidence, "I am safe and confident that I will be well cared for even in the face of frustration."

Jamie's Story

Jamie had been born to a drug-addicted mother. Her childhood environment was chaotic and unsafe. When her mother was finally busted for drug use and imprisoned, Jamie was put into the foster care system and went from one abusive or neglectful environment to the next. It is a miracle that Jamie survived, and she not only survived, but she went on to do well in school, graduate college, get married, and have a blended family with five children. When we met Jamie, she had walls around her heart as thick as any fortress. With good reason, Jamie did not trust anyone to take care of her. She'd never experienced true attachment with a loving caregiver and survived by being smart and mean. You can imagine how this affected her marriage.

Stage 2: Autonomy

The second stage of life, the toddler years, is characterized by the beginnings of independence. If you were not given a safe environment during this stage of development, you will be left with feelings of shame, inadequacy, self-doubt, and a burgeoning rebellious spirit. An adult who was well cared for in this stage of life can say with confidence, "I am valuable and can face the challenges of life, both the victories and the failures."

Thomas's Story

Thomas was born to a single mother. While she loved him the best she could, Thomas longed for a father figure who never showed up. It comes as no surprise that Thomas had severe anger issues that came from feeling utterly and unfairly abandoned. Thomas sought self-worth by excelling in sports—always with one eye on the sidelines, hoping against hope that his father would show up to validate his worth.

Stage 3: Initiative

Between the ages of about three and five, we begin to develop a sense of initiative. A disruption in the child's life at this stage can result in a guilt-ridden adult with low self-esteem who will limit risk, which limits potential. Without initiative, the adult becomes a follower and may be overly dependent in relationships. An adult who had success in this stage of life can say with confidence, "I am capable and can act on my own creative impulses."

Sharon's Story

Sharon's father was a violent man. He beat her mother and raped her repeatedly, and ruled his home with an iron fist. The beatings were so severe that her pregnant mother miscarried her second child. Eventually, her dad deserted them.

Sharon's sympathetic nature served her well as she pursued a career in teaching, but her career growth was stunted by her fearful tendency to be a follower and not a leader. She was quick to obey, but when a decision required creative thinking and initiative, Sharon would shrink back.

Stage 4: Competence

Between the ages of six and twelve we're developing a sense of competence—or incompetence, depending on the quality of support and encouragement we receive. If you lack self-confidence, it will compromise your ability to achieve goals. Arrogance is often the flimsy veil over a deep sense of inferiority. Success in this stage of life creates an adult who can say with confidence, "I am gifted and will use my gifts to create the life I dream of."

Adam's Story

Adam's parents divorced when he was eight years old, and the pain that both of the parents experienced in the process left little room to attend to their youngest child. Adam had some leadership potential that was compromised at an early age and left him feeling guilty and insecure. As a result, he swings wildly between being mouthy, self-righteous, and strongly opinionated to being apologetic and guilty for speaking up. He might strongly challenge and argue with someone's position and then retreat to "just kidding." The wild swings between initiative and guilt cause people, particularly his wife, to dismiss him when he speaks.

Stage 5: Identity

In adolescence we face the critical life challenge of developing a strong identity, an identity that will be the launching pad for finding purpose and direction in life as an adult. A disruption at this stage of life can lead to a compromised self-image, which may create a workaholic, or the opposite, an unmotivated slacker. Confusion and black-and-white thinking characterize both extremes. An adult who has navigated this stage well can say with confidence, "I am unique and whole and have a plan to achieve happiness."

Jim's Story

I experienced two traumatic accidents in my early teens: A fishing mishap put me in intensive care for a week and left me with a punctured retina and double vision, and a fractured femur sidelined me for six months. Up until then, I had been a star athlete, stronger and faster than most of the kids in my age group, but after the broken leg, I never recovered my edge. My self-image was tied up in competitive sports, so when that was no longer an option, I turned, naturally, to chasing girls. But having been sexually abused as a child haunted my relationships. I was filled with sexual shame and self-loathing, and felt lost. I was successful in college and married the most beautiful girl on campus, but my sense of emptiness never really left me. I spent the next couple of decades trying to fill the emptiness and build self-esteem through work. I became a very successful entrepreneur, developing many firsts, from the first teeth-whitening system to the first vitamin-infused soda, but my sense of identity never cohered. Some friends tricked me into going to a Dr. Phil seminar, and that was the beginning of a new growth path. This new growth path included many highs and lows, including divorce, and eventually led me to develop the Marriage Boot Camp.

Stage 6: Intimacy

The sixth stage of life, between the ages of twenty and twenty-five, is a time of forming intimate adult relationships. But if any of the developmental milestones have been compromised along the way, relationships will be a struggle. Most of the people we see in the Marriage Boot Camp fall into this stage of developmental deficit. Our work at the Marriage Boot Camp is to help them to go back and heal some of the wounds from the past. We use games, drills, and exercises to bring the hidden, unconscious wounding to the surface so that it can be dealt with in the present. An adult with a solid foundation built in this stage can say with confidence, "I am loving and lovable and have a desire for intimacy in all of my relationships."

Stage 7: Generativity

In middle adulthood, from twenty-six to sixty-four years old, our need is to create, nurture, or give back. A failure to find ways to contribute can leave a person feeling disconnected and useless. We believe that many marriages stagnate at this point in life because of a flawed view of retirement. Adults who successfully navigate this stage of life can say with confidence, "I am grateful for the life I have and want to give back."

Stage 8: Integrity

The senior years, from the age of sixty-five until death, are a time of looking back and assessing your legacy. A well-lived life results in an adult who can say with confidence, "I am content, have no regrets, have been a success in love and life and have no fear of death."

Virtually every child who has been neglected or abused thinks that their pain and suffering are their fault. This often fills them with shame and is one of the reasons that they bury the pain. Ask any victim of child sexual abuse and he will tell you that deep down he feels responsible for the abuse. It is crucial to realize that your early developmental needs *should have been met by an adult caregiver* and you are not responsible.

Moreover, developmental deficits are not destiny. They can be addressed at any time—and we suggest that now is the time.

Engaging Your Mate

Now that you've read through the developmental stages as they relate to your own life, share this information with your mate. Sharing stories has a way of deepening the bond between partners. Discuss any epiphanies that you have had about when you might have been wounded or were left unsupported. Look back at your life maps together and continue the conversation; ask your mate to look at his life and share any insights that he might have.

INTEGRATION
a thing which has not been understood
inevitably reappears; like an unlaid ghost,
it cannot rest until the mystery has been
resolved and the spell broken.

—Sigmund Freud, 1909

We now understand that our history impacts our present but doesn't have to affect our future. The question is, what do we have to do in order to stop the cycle? Awareness is always the first step. The ABC drill uncovered some of the beliefs that you hold that may be creating more problems than solutions. These beliefs tie back to something you learned to believe, but when? We did some more excavation, digging into your past by means of exploring your hot buttons and found the source of some of your wounds. Then we had you draw out your personal life map to illustrate more of your history and where your developmental deficits might have come from. This should give you a great starting point for the next step in our journey: integration.

Integration is one of the hardest exercises we will ask you to do. It requires that you embrace the things that you have buried and avoided as a means of surviving but whose avoidance is now doing you more harm than good.

Many of us are damaged as children, and this damage results in negative traits and behaviors that show up in our current relationships. But we don't realize it because we have unconsciously buried the part of us that is wounded. Buried alive. We push the things that we fear, loathe, and despise in ourselves into the farthest reaches of our unconscious, and yet we are held in bondage by our very fear and disgust. In addition, we continually allocate precious resources toward keeping parts of ourselves hidden. What a waste!

One way to understand this is to imagine that you have an angry, vicious dog that you've locked in the basement and the only way to keep this destructive dog away from you is for you to lean on that basement door to keep the dog at bay. You hate this dog. This dog embarrasses you and you wish it didn't even exist. Holding the door shut has become such a normal part of your life that you don't even realize you are doing it. The angry dog is your split-off, unconscious, wounded self. Even though this unconsciously buried material—the dog in the basement—is deeply repressed, it doesn't stay quiet. It will often show up and sabotage us in its attempt to be heard, particularly during stressful moments. We call this the child-self, because this is usually a part of ourselves that gets split off in childhood, at a time when we didn't have the ability to manage the torrent of emotion. With no other tools, no safe place to process, we bury our pain. The adult-self is the part of us that we are conscious of, our functioning identity, but it is incomplete and depleted by the constant need to hide.

Have you ever wondered why you sometimes behave like an immature child? Do you sometimes say cruel or outrageous things that you immediately regret? Perhaps you can't even believe what's coming out of your mouth and think, "That is so not me!" It's probably your child-self wanting to be heard. Holding the angry, barking dog in the basement while you lean against the door gets harder as we get older. We don't mellow with age like a fine wine; we actually lose some of our youthful defense mechanisms, and we get tired of holding the door shut. Often, bitterness sets in, or worse: All of the poison from the unhealed wound comes spewing out.

Why do we put so much energy into shutting down the child-self? Because the child-self carries shame, guilt, selfish behavior, and addictions. However, it also carries childlike joy, creativity, passion, and the energy of youth. Therefore the best solution isn't to muzzle our child-selves, but to *integrate* the child-self and the adult-self into the real-self. Integration is a result of self-acceptance, self-forgiveness, and self-love.

Integration is a difficult journey that can sometimes take many years in individual psychotherapy, but we can give you a head start. In order to move forward, we often need to go back and look at how we got to where we are today. Everyone wants to be free; we all want to live fully. We are tired of living in fear, tired of faking it and hoping no one knows our true nature. We all want to be free to be who we were designed to be and are tired of living up to some artificial standard. It is deep in our nature, and yet there are things in our lives that hold us in bondage and limit our ability to live abundantly. And who holds the key to your jail cell? You do. What happened in your life that caused you to feel safer locked away than roaming free?

BOOT CAMP CALL TO ACTION

Integration requires that you embrace the things you have hidden down in the basement because they are blocking the full expression of your life force. Integration requires that you open the basement door and let the angry, vicious barking dog out and allow it to express all of its pent-up malice and anger. Each of us has a loud inner critic. Some in the healing arts call this "wrestling with the gremlin," "beast work," or "facing the dragon." You've probably heard the expression "I'm harder on myself than anybody else." It is important to your healing to give this energy a voice. During this step, you're going to note all of your negative internal messages—and it won't be pretty. As if our traumatic experiences weren't enough, the leftover negative beliefs about ourselves have to be wrestled to the ground and defeated. Please find a quiet, private space to do this work. Some of our clients like to drive somewhere, such as to a quiet lakefront or a wooded area, in order to be alone. In any case, bring a photograph of yourself as a child or a hand mirror to look into.

Here are some of Elizabeth's negative beliefs; you may find some of them familiar:

- I am annoying and must keep my mouth shut.
- I am a low-class, ill-bred, mixed-race mutt.
- I'll never be pretty, so I have to be rich to be loved.
- If anyone really knew me, they would hate me.
- I will be accepted only if I can be used.
- I am too serious; I don't know how to have fun.
- Other people's needs are more important than mine.

Begin to see the unconscious parts of "who you are" that are buried and kept out of your consciousness but that pop up at the most inconvenient times. Let these buried thoughts speak freely and feel the self-contempt. Journaling is a great way to unmask the bad tapes. Understand that many of these thoughts run the gamut from truth to fantasy to utter lies, but that is irrelevant. These buried thoughts are a part of your emotional life and don't always fit in the logic box.

During this exercise, you will hear your inner voices clearly because you will actually verbalize all of these condemning words.

Sitting in your quiet space, imagine your inner critic saying, "I hate you because . . ." and fill in the blank with something loathsome that you hear about yourself. Loudly. Each time you say something, you will hit the seat of your chair with your fist or your hand as if you were hitting your child-self. We have also used bats and punching bags to great effect, but if you don't have those at your disposal, be sure that you do something physical but not dangerous. Use your imagination and give the exercise one hundred percent. You have to feel the pain in order to release the pain.

Your statements will sound something like this:

- I hate that you are a liar.
- I hate that you were a nerd.
- I hate that you are a thief.
- I hate that you are damaged goods because you were molested.
- I hate that you're stupid.
- I hate that kids made fun of you at school.
- I hate that you're fat and ugly.
- I hate that you cheated.
- I hate that you are weak.
- I hate you.

Using your deepest emotional language, bring as much energy as you can to this process and really feel the feelings that come up. Push yourself to verbalize every negative belief, everything that you hate about your child-self, everything you are ashamed of, and don't stop until every point has reached the height of its energy. If you are giving one hundred percent, you will be exhausted. When you feel that your inner critic has had his or her say, take a moment and just breathe until your heart rate settles and you are back to being centered in your adult-self. Go ahead and get to it.

Next, switch roles from abuser to abused and imagine that *you* are the child who just got beat up and screamed at. Look into the eyes of your child-self in the photograph you chose or in the hand mirror you brought and replay the malicious, hurtful tapes. Take a moment and feel the pain of the accusations, the unfairness of it all.

Now, as your child-self, imagine that a jury is standing in front of you. Face your photograph toward the jury and defend yourself against the unfair accusations. Explain why you've had to bury your voice, how it wasn't safe for you to be exposed so you had to hide. Defend yourself and show them that this wasn't your fault even if you still believe that it is. Know this: IT IS NOT YOUR FAULT. Every child deserves to be well cared for and made to feel safe, lovable, and valuable, and if you do not feel this, it is not your fault. Go ahead and say it out loud: "It is not my fault that I did not feel safe."

Even though you *understand* that you were an innocent child, you still feel guilty, don't you? You feel the false guilt, the shame. "It's my fault that I was molested, abused, and mistreated." Can you ever forgive yourself for being a failure? For acting out in your pain? For being destructive and angry? Continue imagining that you are the beat-up child. Now imagine that your adult-self has replaced the jury and is standing in front of you, staring at you. Look into your adult face and plead for mercy, grace, and love from the adult you. Beg for compassion and forgiveness for everything you feel ashamed of or guilty for. Ask your adult-self to set you free, to love you, and to take care of you.

Now switch points of view to your adult-self and imagine that you are looking into the face of your child-self, who just begged for mercy, grace, love, and forgiveness. Can you see the hurt and pain in her eyes? It's time to release her from her past mistakes. It's time to forgive your child-self so that you can move forward in life and love yourself. It's time to integrate the two of you so that you can grow together. Begin with the condemning tape and replace it with a grace-filled truth.

Start with one item on your list and say, "You are not_____; in fact, you are_____ . . ." while imagining your own child-self.

Continue going through your shame list until you reach the end. Here are some examples of what you might say:

- "You are not unlovable. You are truly worthy of love."
- "You are not fat and disgusting. You are beautiful and unique."
- "You are not a liar. You were protecting yourself."
- "You are not to blame for being molested. You were vulnerable and should have been protected."

Imagine your child-self in front of you crying, pleading for your compassion. Pleading to be let out of the basement and into your life.

Hold out your arms in front of you. Hold them there until they start to ache and you are ready to embrace your child-self. When you are ready, imagine that you are wrapping your arms around this child and hugging him or her to your chest and onto your lap. You have your arms around him. Commit to your child-self to take care of him and to help him fight the condemning voices for the rest of your life. Commit to being patient and kind and loving. Pull him in to your chest and give him a tight hug. Hold the hug.

Hug your child-self tighter. Allow him to melt completely into you. Ask yourself the following:

- Who are your arms around now?
- Who do you love now?
- Who have you forgiven?

IT'S YOU!

Repeat these phrases as you hold yourself in a safe embrace:

- From now on I will always defend myself against the inner critic.
- From now on I will have mercy and grace for myself.
- From now on I will have compassion for myself.
- I love myself.
- I love myself. (Yes, say it again.)

This process will take time and may need to be revisited. In fact, it is our hope that you continue to dialogue with your child-self for the rest of your life. The objective of this drill is to develop what we call the "inner nurturer"—the voice of comfort when you come under stress or attack. You must develop nurturing affirmations that combat the voices of shame, and you must work to shut off the condemning recordings that play in your head. Imagine that you are a nurturing parent and are soothing a suffering child. Here is what you might sound like:

CONDEMNER: "How could you be so stupid? You are such a fool!"

NURTURER: "You're still growing and learning. Don't be so hard on yourself. Look how far you've come!"

CONDEMNER: "God, you're so fat!"

NURTURER: "No, you are beautiful and unique and worthy of love just the way you are."

CONDEMNER: "If anyone found out the truth, they would hate you!"

NURTURER: "The more real you are, the more lovable you are. You don't need the approval of haters."

CONDEMNER: "You are a loser and will never make it!"

NURTURER: "You are built for excellence, not perfection. You will never stop reaching and growing."

CONDEMNER: "Why do you have to think so much?"

NURTURER: "Your mind is a beautiful thing and should be free to move at its own pace."

Your primary caregiver should've provided this voice when you were young and vulnerable, but it's not impossible to develop it even now.

Elizabeth's Story

Not only did I spend a great deal of time getting an advanced education in psychology, but I was also in psychotherapy for fifteen years (a luxury that few of us can afford, but I was blessed with great health insurance, two amazing therapists, and a relationship with God that changed my life). I did not have any inner nurturing voices, only critics. Every day felt like a beatdown, which I covered over with narcissistic, grandiose lies, professional achievements, and denial. These counterfeits ended up costing me much more than they were giving me. Every achievement made me feel that my value was in performance; every grandiose lie increased my self-loathing, because deep down, I still felt like a failure and a fake. I had to do the hard work of integration. I had to start accepting the real me and make peace with the truth of who I was. I had the help of some amazing healers. My healers not only filled me with a sense of their delight in me, but their confidence in me was strong enough to be internalized and I carry their voices around with me every day. Here are just a few examples of my unique nurturing voices:

- You are wonderfully and fearfully made. You are the exact design that was planned.
- You are not overly analytical; I love the way your mind works!
- Asking you to stop using your mind in the way that you do would be like asking an elephant to stop using its trunk.

These voices still bring tears of gratitude to my heart, and yours will, too. An inner nurturing voice is life-giving!

Engaging Your Mate

Now that you've walked through the difficult process of integration, share this information with your mate and any epiphanies that you have about your own inner critic and your child-self. Ask your mate if they have any negative messages rolling around in his or her head that may need to be put to rest.

BONDING WITH YOUR MATE

Putting the past in the past can be wonderfully healing for every individual; however, the greatest reward is for the relationship. In order to have a deep, intimate relationship with another human being, it is necessary to be real and transparent. The degree of your authenticity is the degree of intimacy and bonding that you can achieve.

While we at Marriage Boot Camp are big believers in having great relational skills like communication, conflict management, and conflict resolution, nothing is more important than having a powerful bond with your spouse. Without this bond, no amount of skill will give you the kind of joy-filled and life-giving marriage that we are all meant to have.

Our culture, which values independence so highly, has managed to take a healthy view of attachment and turn it into something that we are supposed to grow out of when we become adults—not so! It is not good for mankind to be alone. We were never meant to live in isolation, and the fear of being alone can be found in every human heart. In fact, many studies link the quality of our intimate relationships with physical health. Neurobiology identifies specific chemicals that come from connection, such as the "cuddle hormone" oxytocin, which protects us from both physical and psychological disease.

Jim and Elizabeth's Story

For years Jim and Elizabeth went merrily through life, happy in love, in marriage, and in ministry. After a series of bad relationships and a devastating divorce, Elizabeth felt safe for the first time in her life.

Then we hit a speed bump. Our once "perfect" marriage erupted in conflict in a way neither one of us saw coming. What we discovered, to our surprise, was that we both have attachment issues that had never come to light because life had been working really well for us.

When Elizabeth feels threatened, she shuts down and becomes cold, with the aim of guarding her heart. Jim, on the other hand, responds to conflict by chasing Elizabeth down, tackling her, and demanding attention and love. That didn't work out so well. The more self-protective and aloof Elizabeth became, the more Jim pursued her, and the more he pursued her, the more she ran away. Around and around they went. In other words, Elizabeth has an *avoidant attachment* style under stress and Jim has an *anxious attachment* style under stress. It was only when we recognized this essential difference that we were able to work out our conflict.

The purpose of this next exercise is to discover what attachment and bonding look like to you and to your mate and to give you some tools to repair breaches in this bond when they occur.

Engaging Your Mate

During this sharing session, you'll be speaking from your heart and doing your best to be open and authentic. Remember the very basic rules of the share session:

- When one person is talking, the other is listening.
- Do not give advice.
- Do not analyze.
- Do not judge.
- Never use what a person shares against him.
- Mirror back what you heard and share how it makes you feel.

Now for the work. Take turns sharing your thoughts on each of the points below. Do *not* engage in a tit for tat. While your mate speaks, put your thoughts, feelings, and opinions on hold. There should never be recriminations for the feelings you express. This has to be a safe conversation from your heart.

Share with your mate . . .

- how you feel about depending on him or her
- your description of an ideal bonded relationship
- the things you do to try to engage your mate
- the things you do to distance yourself from your mate
- how you would you like your mate to respond when you reach out
- the ways you feel your mate pushes you away
- how you feel when you experience that rejection
- what you do when you feel rejected

Now that you have this information about each other, do you see a pattern of bonding and rejection? Common patterns include pursue/withdraw, attack/avoid, complaint/countercomplaint, attack/

defend. Try to identify which pattern the two of you have and take a moment to share your thoughts. Once you have identified the pattern, slow the narrative down and then try to identify the steps in the process that lead to escalation.

Jim and Elizabeth's Pattern

As you saw, we fall into the classic pursue-withdraw pattern. When one of us gets hurt, we respond with our old ingrained behaviors. Elizabeth withdraws and Jim pursues. Elizabeth withdraws more, and Jim pursues harder. To break the cycle, we have learned to invoke an attachment-repair strategy that looks like this: Affirm, validate, acknowledge your part, then problem solve. Once one of the partners becomes aware of the cycle or recognizes that they offended their mate, they should invoke the repair strategy. Here is an example of the repair strategy from two different perspectives:

Jim's POV: "I notice that we are wrapped around the axle. Let's slow things down and try to reconnect." Affirm: "I really want us to feel close again, and I realize that I hurt you." Validate: "I understand that you are withdrawing from me to protect yourself, not to reject me." Acknowledge your part: "But honestly, it feels like rejection, and it takes everything in my power not to chase you down and try to force you to get over your hurt. I'm sorry that I hurt you." Problem solve: "What can we do to put a salve on the hurt?"

Elizabeth's POV: "It seems like we're not making progress. Let's slow things down and try to reconnect." Affirm: "I really want us to feel close again, and I realize that I hurt you." Validate: "I understand that your natural response is to pursue me and try to hurt me like you feel hurt." Acknowledge my part: "And when this happens, my natural response is to withdraw." Problem solve: "We both know that we want to reconnect, so what do we need to do to put a salve on the hurt?"

At this point a frank and vulnerable conversation about what each person needs is the beginning of the end of the conflict. Each party needs to get clarity on what their unique "salve" looks like and be prepared to share that, and also must be willing to be the healing agent their mate needs them to be.

This sets you up to problem solve in a productive way. Once you have cleared out the cobwebs from your past, you may want to revisit the section on conflict resolution in chapter eight and use our step-by-step method of negotiating conflict. Changing the patterns that disrupt our attachment to our mate means putting the past in the past.

In summary, we first have to humbly understand that we all bring baggage from our past to our relationships in ways that disrupt our attachment. Then we have to identify our wounds and understand where they came from, replace our inner voices, and forgive ourselves. We then have to recognize when our mate hits one of our hot buttons and we get triggered. Finally, we have to commit to repairing the bond of love in our relationships, forgive, and make a commitment to always be growing together. In the next chapter, we will discuss forgiveness and how to use this powerful tool to renew the freshness of first love.

KEY TAKEAWAYS FOR THIS CHAPTER

- Before we go forward, we often have to look back.
- There are specific developmental milestones that we must achieve as we grow, and if we fail, we carry the deficit forward.
- Childhood deficits often get boxed up and hidden, and it is our job to open that box and heal the wounds rather than avoid them.
- Each of us brings baggage to the marriage and it must be responsibly and compassionately managed.
- Unhealed wounds from childhood (baggage) often show up in our marriages and can destroy the bond of love.

10

....

THE NEED FOR FORGIVENESS

....

 **QUICK QUIZ** Is your marriage all that you dreamed it would be? Have you and your mate become more roommates than lovers? Do you long for those times in the beginning when you felt like your spouse was your soul mate and your best friend? Do you worry that you just don't love each other anymore?

One of the most common reasons that people come to the Marriage Boot Camp, they tell us, is that they've lost the love in their relationship and are considering divorce. For many people, the loss of love marks the end of the marriage, but for us it can be the beginning of a brand-new relationship with more depth and intimacy than you can imagine.

How can that be? Because most of the time when we start to dig into this problem, we find a root of bitterness. Something happened, someone got hurt, it was never addressed, and the hurt got swept under the rug. Nothing kills the heart faster than an unresolved heartache. Believe it or not, the best way to bring a dead relationship back to life is one simple tool: forgiveness.

Richard and Alice's Story

Richard and Alice were in their sixties and had been married for more than thirty years when they came to the Marriage Boot Camp. They had been living as virtual roommates for their entire marriage. Neither one of them believed in divorce, so they just hung in there, decade after decade, living in silent, polite misery. They did manage to have four children along the way, who eventually intervened and forced them to come to the Marriage Boot Camp. Their children—now adults—saw how miserable they were and wanted so much more for them.

It was clear that Richard did not want to be there. To make things worse, Alice had told him that it was just for two days when, actually, it's a four-day program. She also allowed him to believe that it would be a small private experience, so when he walked into a room of one hundred and fifty people, his face turned bright red with anger. He made it very clear from the get-go that he was pissed as hell at being tricked into this experience and wanted to leave but couldn't because their airline tickets were nonrefundable.

"I don't love my wife, I haven't loved my wife for the past twenty-eight years, and nothing you can say is going to change that. I've stayed in this marriage for our children and to honor my vows," Richard announced to the room at large. Alice just hung her head and nodded because this was not news to her.

Her shame and pain filled the room, and we looked at each other, thinking, "This couple is going to be one of the few who don't make it through Marriage Boot Camp."

How did Richard and Alice's marriage become so strained? The problem was a root of bitterness that was allowed to grow and fester. Alice had hidden a prior marriage from Richard, and Richard was never able to get past the betrayal. He told her that she had lied to him, and he considered her "damaged goods" because she wasn't a virgin when they married. He held on to Alice's violation against the marriage and retaliated by getting rid of her beloved dog (given to her by her first husband) and claimed that now they were even—an eye for an eye. The problem was that neither one of them truly felt like the books were balanced. Richard believed that Alice's "sin" was greater than his, and Alice felt that Richard's "sin" was much worse. Alice would point out that getting rid of her dog was much worse since her "sin" was to protect him from the hurt and also to protect her own pride. She pointed out that Richard's "sin" was not only mean-spirited and unnecessary, but also vindictive, to which he would respond that his action was to take the anger out of the marriage by making sure that proper "penance" was being paid. Both lived with this "balance," but despite the attempt at a solution, neither one of them felt close, connected, or loved.

What Richard and Alice both had to learn was the skill of forgiveness, both toward those who have harmed you and for yourself when you have fallen short of your own standards.

FORGIVENESS—WHAT IT IS AND WHAT IT ISN'T

Leftover anger can metastasize into a bitter, silent cancer that makes a healthy relationship almost impossible. How do we get rid of it? We've read a lot of theories on how to get rid of bitterness, but our experience with thousands of couples has shown us there is only one real answer. That answer is forgiveness. We're not talking about the superficial, self-righteous forgiveness that makes you feel superior. Nor are we talking about letting someone off the hook and avoiding the issues. We're talking about hard-core, gut-wrenching forgiveness, where you enter into the pain and choose to release it all.

It is said that unforgiveness is like drinking poison and hoping that someone else dies. Stop drinking the poison. Forgiveness is hard work, but it's well worth the effort. Research shows that one of the keys to having a long-term happy marriage is the art of forgiveness. No matter how good you are at relationships, you'll never be perfect, and the only way to deal with those moments of imperfection, much less those moments of extreme failure, is forgiveness.

What Is Your Definition of Forgiveness?

Take a moment to try to answer this question off the top of your head. Do you see unforgiveness as the moral high ground, the place from which you can look down on the bad guys? Many of us were taught this. Does forgiveness mean that after you've accepted the apology, you can never bring up the issue again? When you tell your mate, "I forgive you," do you silently add "but I won't forget this"? Do you say you forgive but find yourself bringing up the issue during a conflict about something unrelated and get mad all over again?

The Marriage Boot Camp definition of forgiveness: Forgiveness is acknowledging that someone has caused you harm, resulting in bitterness that continues to this day, and then choosing to release that person from any form of payment or revenge, now and forevermore.

This definition has probably left you with a lot of unanswered questions, so let's dive a little deeper into the definition and give you some answers.

Is Forgiveness a Decision?

Yes. Forgiveness is a decision. It is a decision to say no to the natural desire to repay a hurt for a hurt. This is often a difficult first step because you will have to revisit the hurt. While revisiting the pain, you have to make a decision to not repay a hurt for a hurt. It may actually seem like you are paying for something that the offender should be paying for. Hang in there. There is freedom at the end of this journey.

Is There Anyone Who Doesn't Deserve Forgiveness?

No, because forgiveness is for *you*, not the person who hurt you. The truth is, he doesn't even have to know! When you forgive, it frees *you*, not the person you're forgiving.

Does Forgiveness Mean You Are Condoning, Excusing, or Denying an Offense?

Sometimes it feels like it, doesn't it? Many people believe that if you forgive someone, like your spouse, you are excusing bad behavior or letting the offender off the hook. But depending on the circumstances, you can forgive and still prosecute someone to the fullest extent of the law. Forgiveness is an act of the heart and mind, not an act of law enforcement.

Imagine that you got mad at me and decided to key my car. Can I forgive you? Yes. Can I forgive you *and* make you pay for the repair? Yes. I can choose both to forgive you by saying no to the impulse to key your car in return and still hold you accountable to pay the penalty for scratching my car. Now, I could also expect you to suffer the consequences of your behavior without forgiving you; but when I forgive you, I can sleep soundly because I have released you from my heart and mind.

How Many Times Must You Forgive?

The answer is, as many times as it takes. The first time is the hardest. You must choose to forgive each time the issue comes up.

Let's go back to scratching my car. I forgave you when you scratched my car. I went to bed without any anger toward you. The next morning when I go out to get in my car, I'm going to get mad again. Yes. The anger has come back. So, I'll forgive you again. Then, when I take my car to the shop for repairs and they show me the estimate, I'll forgive you again. Then, when they give me the cheap rental car, I'll have to forgive you again. When the paint job doesn't match up perfectly, I'll have to forgive you again. I'll have to forgive you as many times as it takes. Why? Because forgiveness is for *me*.

Do You Have to Forget?

"Forgive and forget" sounds really good in theory, but in real life, only truly minor offenses can be forgotten. Can you really forget that you were molested, that you were bullied in school, or that your business partner stole from you? No. Our minds are not capable of forgetting such pain. If forgetting were a condition of forgiveness, we would all be stuck with unforgiveness.

Doesn't Forgiveness Mean "Giving In"?

Does the bad guy win if you forgive him? No! Frankly, the people you haven't forgiven hold the cards. We like to think we do, because we have the power to forgive or not to forgive. In reality, they have control because they are living rent-free in your head, and the only way you can take control back is to release them by forgiving.

Does Forgiveness Break Generations of Damage?

Yes. How many of you ended up with traits from your parents that you didn't want? Unforgiveness traps you into being something that you don't want to be.

Does Unforgiveness Block Healing and Growth?

Yes. Think about it: You build walls to protect yourself from being hurt again, and those same walls keep you from being able to accept and give love freely. Imagine that you have a limited supply of life resources (time, energy, memory, attention, creativity). Choosing not to forgive means that you have allocated a portion of your life resources to maintaining your walls and your "unforgiveness" account. Why allocate any of your life resources to the person who has done you the most harm? When those resources are freed up, they can be reallocated for love, growth, and productivity.

Does Unforgiveness Cause You to Live in the Past?

Unless you forgive, you remain stuck in the time and place of the offense. Unforgiveness keeps the past in your present by allowing it to sit subconsciously on your to-do list.

If You Refuse to Forgive, Are You Out of God's Will?

Almost all religions say yes, you are out of the will of God if you do not forgive others. Forgiveness requires that you take yourself out of the revenge loop by making the decision to not repay an evil with another evil. If you live by unforgiveness, you will be the target of unforgiveness. Do unto others as you would have them do unto you.

What Is the Difference Between Forgiving Someone from Your Past and Someone You're Currently in a Relationship With?

Now, this is when things get real. As we saw with Richard and Alice, being in a relationship with someone who has offended you requires a much deeper level of forgiveness. We call this reconciliation, and reconciliation requires the participation of the person you want to be in a relationship with. Forgiveness with reconciliation clears the air between two people and can repair the bond that was broken by an offense.

Do You Have to Confront the Offender?

No, you don't have to confront the person who hurt you. You can make the decision to forgive and move on, and in fact, confrontation might do more harm than good. You must, however, acknowledge your pain and be brutally honest with yourself and perhaps with a trusted confidant before you can completely release the offender.

If, on the other hand, you want a deep, intimate relationship with this person, the answer is yes, you do have to confront the offender, but in a loving way. Confronting the offender means confessing your feelings of pain. Skill is required on both sides of this equation. You must get in touch with your deep, vulnerable feelings, not just the anger, and share them in a way that doesn't feel like an attack. On the other side, the offender must be willing and able to hear your heart in a loving way that does not include defensiveness or justification. The offender must be able to mirror your feelings back accurately. This opens the door to repairing the bond of friendship, but you can still decide, even after clearing the air, that it's not good for you to have this person in your life. That is your choice.

Does the Other Person Have to Apologize?

Wouldn't it be great if your offender came to you and begged for your forgiveness? It's their job, right? If only! Outside of a close relationship, this will probably never happen. The idea of "justice" or "fairness" has to be taken out of the forgiveness equation. For your own sake, get rid of the extra weight you've been carrying on your shoulders and choose to let go of the burden of balancing the books with a hurt for a hurt.

If, on the other hand, you want a relationship with this person, the answer changes because the goal includes repairing the closeness. There are many unique ways to repair closeness, and an apology is often one of them. The key is that the offender must understand your feelings and want to stop the behavior that causes you pain.

Do the People Who Have Hurt You Need to Understand What They Did?

No. They don't even have to know that you are thinking about them! They also don't have to care that they hurt you (unless you want to be in a relationship with the offender). Many people get this confused. They think to themselves that they will finally be able to release the person who did them harm if they could only show them what they did. Not even close. Someone who doesn't care about you will not be open to hearing your pain, and sharing it with them may even make it worse. But within a loving relationship, not only does the offender have to truly understand how they hurt you, but you must be convinced and confident that they understand you.

THE TWO TYPES OF FORGIVENESS

As we saw with the last few questions, your definition of forgiveness depends on whether or not you want to be in a relationship with the person who has done you harm. There are certain people who have hurt us who should not be allowed in our lives! Because of this, there are two levels of forgiveness, each with a different impact on your relationships.

Level-One Forgiveness

Level-one forgiveness says, "I will not repay evil for evil." This does not come naturally. Deep down inside each of us is a spirit of justice that wants to mete out an eye for an eye and a tooth for a tooth. It's very natural to feel that way, but we also know that to *act* on that desire often gets us in more trouble than it's worth. Thus we have to choose not to retaliate. Level-one forgiveness is an absolute necessity if you want to be emotionally healthy. Level-one forgiveness is an absolute necessity if you want to fulfill the biblical command to forgive. Level-one forgiveness is a requirement whether or not you want to be in a relationship with the person who has done you harm.

Level-Two Forgiveness

When you want to remain in or rekindle a relationship with someone who has harmed you, you need to practice level-two forgiveness, or reconciliation. Reconciliation is forgiveness taken to a deeper level, and it's more complicated because it requires the cooperation of the person who has offended you. According to Dr. Mark Baker, executive director of La Vie Counseling Centers in Pasadena, California, clinical psychologist, and marriage and family counselor, forgiveness that results in reconciliation requires three things:

1. Reconciliation begins with a vulnerable acknowledgment of your feelings. It's not enough to say that you're angry; you have to go deeper and express your hurt, your fear, your frustration, and your shame. This may be more difficult than it seems. Deeply buried hurt and pain often reside in the subconscious, away from conscious thought, simply because they are too painful to have to live with on a day-to-day basis. You can find clues to this deeply buried pain because it shows up sometimes in your dreams and sometimes as a hot button. At the Marriage Boot Camp we use role-playing, a powerful tool to help people get in touch with the deeper feelings surrounding the wound.

2. Reconciliation also requires that the offending party understand your feelings such that they no longer want to continue the behavior that caused you harm. This cannot become a conversation of who's right and who's wrong, because frankly, it doesn't matter. What does matter is that

the offending party has empathy and can honestly say, "I don't want to make you feel this kind of pain, so I'm going to do things differently in the future."

3. Finally, reconciliation requires that you truly believe the offender grasps the pain they have caused. You have to believe that you are seen, heard, and understood and that the person you are in the relationship with actually cares how you feel.

When these three things take place in the forgiveness process, then reconciliation can happen at a deep level, and that is the goal in the Marriage Boot Camp. When two people come back from hurting each other and reconnect in a bond of love, that love can be even stronger than before the offense.

BOOT CAMP CALL TO ACTION—PART I

Now is the time to put what you've learned into practice. We're going to start small. Find a quiet place where you can have complete privacy. We want you to think about someone *other than your mate* who has hurt you in the past.

Elizabeth's Story

I guess at ten years old I must have had a pretty smart mouth, because I remember my fifth-grade math teacher taking me out in the hallway during class and shoving me against the metal lockers while screaming at me. I was quite tiny, probably no more than sixty pounds, so in retrospect his behavior seems monstrous. I was terrified and felt completely violated as well as guilty and frightened. As an adult I was able to write this incident off as the stupidity of an unstable man, but if I were being honest, I was still mad at him. Despite the fact that I had no interest in the man and didn't even know if he was still alive, I finally realized it was flavoring my attitude toward men in authority. Investing even a little bit of energy toward someone so insignificant in my life meant I had some work to do.

Ask yourself the following questions:

How are you hurting yourself by not forgiving?
For me, the problem was the disrespect for men I developed early in my life. This disrespect was hurting my relationship with my husband, and I also was wasting life resources by keeping this old debt on my subconscious ledger.

What lies do you believe that are keeping you from forgiving?
The lie that I believed was that this man did not deserve to be forgiven. I believed that forgiveness was a gift and refused to give it to a bad person who didn't deserve it. This leftover bitterness I carry inside me caused me to think deep down that all men are stupid, lack self-control, and cannot be trusted.

How are you damaging yourself by choosing to hold on to anger, bitterness, and resentment?
Holding on to my anger over this incident kept me from loving with my whole heart. It created an unconscious wall between those I love and myself.

What would be different about your life if you were able to let go?

If I were able to completely forgive and let go of this incident, I would get my whole heart back and be able to give and receive love freely.

Use Your Imagination

Now it's time to use your imagination and put yourself into the situation that caused you pain. Stop and take a moment to search through your memory banks. Once you have the memory in your mind, read on.

Imagine that the anger, bitterness, and resentment that you feel is actually a heavy weight pressing down on your shoulders. The person who hurt you is placing this burden on you, and the weight is unforgiveness. Do you really want to carry it?

Imagine in addition to the weight on your shoulders that you have a knot in your stomach. It twists tighter and tighter every day because you refuse to release it. That knot is unforgiveness. Why are you hanging on to it?

You decide to run from it, but something is holding your feet. You can't move forward and you can't get up. What would it feel like to be free?

Suddenly you feel constricted. Your chest tightens and you have a difficult time breathing. You look down and notice ropes wound around your chest that tie you to your chair. The more you think about the anger and hurt, the tighter the ropes pull. The ropes are your unforgiveness. How will you survive?

As you struggle, you notice a warm, brilliant flame of unconditional love glowing just ten feet in front of you. You try to get to it, but you are unable to move, and there is something between you and the light, a wall of bulletproof glass. The wall is your unforgiveness. This wall is blocking you from the unconditional love.

Are you ready to tear down the wall of unforgiveness? Are you tired of being a slave to your abuser? You decided long ago *not* to forgive. You can now make the decision *to forgive*. However, you must revisit the pain.

You make the decision to start the journey, and the image beyond the bulletproof glass comes into focus. The person who abused you is sitting on the other side, but the wall in front of you suddenly turns into prison bars and the jailhouse comes into focus. You realize that *you* are the one in prison, and your abuser is on the outside laughing at you. He can't believe how stupid you are for putting yourself in jail for something he did. Feel your anger and hurt toward this person. Feel the injustice.

Imagine him saying the following things to you:

- Forgive me for what? You were the one in the wrong.
- You deserved what you got.
- It wasn't my fault. You caused me to do it.
- You're so stupid. You don't even know how to forgive.
- I don't want your forgiveness. You keep it.
- I have control over you. You have empowered me.
- Get over it. You're acting like a baby.
- I don't care; you're only hurting yourself.
- I never cared about you anyway.

Go ahead and feel your rage, your helplessness. It may be uncomfortable, but it's important that you get really deep in your vulnerable feelings. If you are giving one hundred percent, your emotions should be stirred up.

BOOT CAMP CALL TO ACTION—PART II

We are now going to have you utilize a psychotherapeutic technique called "Gestalt" or "empty chair." In this exercise, you will imagine the person you need to forgive in an empty chair in front of you. This may feel awkward at first, but it is a time-tested, proven technique to help you heal.

To truly forgive someone, you must feel the hurt and pain again. You can't just release the hurt in your head; you have to release it in your heart. Dig really deep and use the power of your imagination. The deeper you go, the deeper the healing will be. You've probably seen us do this exercise with the boot campers on the television show. This can be a very real, very deep experience to finally say the things you've always wanted to say to the person who hurt you. This is a good time to journal your responses.

- Tell the offender how he hurt you. Say everything that you need to say to him with as much detail and feeling as you can muster. Imagine him mocking you.
- Tell him how the offense has made you feel about yourself. Imagine his uncaring spirit.
- Tell him how the offense has affected your life, your marriage, and even your children.

Now it is time to let go of the hurt and anger. Start with something small, like "I forgive you for your uncaring spirit." Repeat it over and over until it becomes real for you and you feel a bit of release from the hurt deep inside.

Now pick a larger offense that you need to forgive. Then take a deep breath and hold it while you think about the offense. Doesn't it feel unnatural? That is what unforgiveness does to you. Hold your breath until you can't hold it any longer, then let the breath out and say, "I forgive you for _____."

Work through your list of offenses and verbalize your forgiveness, point by point. Do not move on until you have sincerely released the offender.

Now, really see the offender in your mind's eye and make the decision to forgive that person for *everything*. It's time to release all the buried emotion.

Take a deep breath and hold it. When you are ready to forgive, release the breath and say, "I forgive you for everything." Say it a minimum of five times, taking as much time as you need. When you are ready, we will go on to the next part of this process.

All right, now switch chairs (yes, we know the other chair is empty, but do it anyway) and imagine that *you are the offending person* looking into your face in the empty chair. Take a moment to imagine that you are looking into your own face, and speaking directly to yourself, say the following:

- I'm sorry.
- I now understand the pain that I caused you.
- You are right; your pain is very real.
- Please forgive me.

Take a moment to come up with whatever phrase your heart wants to hear from the person who hurt you, and say those exact words.

Once you have finished role-playing the offender, switch seats again and settle into your own identity. What are you feeling in your heart? Did you do it? Did you release your abuser? You should be feeling lighter, more at peace. Don't be surprised to feel something of a void or a kind of emptiness—that's a normal result of getting rid of the weight of unforgiveness. Fill it with love and compassion. This is the beauty of forgiveness; you are now free to love in a way that you have never been able to before. How can you know if you have truly forgiven someone? The answer is that you can now wish them well. You have released them from your mental penitentiary, and they are free to live their life as you are free to go on with yours without them.

Repeat this process for everyone in your life that you are holding in the prison of your heart, and free yourself of every bitter root. Remember, forgiveness is for you, and it is something you will have to do over and over. Just know that each time, you gain a little more freedom, and eventually forgiveness will become as natural as breathing.

Elizabeth's Story

I had to forgive my fifth-grade math teacher. Just the thought of him continuing to press down on my life was motivation enough to get rid of him. I imagined standing out in the hallway of Franklin Elementary School with him yelling at me and pushing me against the lockers. I felt my fear, humiliation, and anger. I imagined throwing him in jail and telling him that he was a pathetic little man who couldn't control his temper. I told him that his abuse caused me to see all men as pathetic creatures who could not be trusted because they would hurt me. I said many other things that I simply won't put in print.

Then I imagined that I was the one in jail and it was time to set myself free. I sat in the other chair and imagined that I was him. I looked at this tearstained little face and I was horrified at my behavior. I heard him say to me, "What I did to you was wrong, and worse, what I said about you was wrong. Please forgive me so that you can be free."

I didn't need to switch chairs again. I had released my teacher and forgiven him completely. I now have only compassion for this man, because I believe that he must have been tormented to do such a horrible thing, and I imagined that he now knew that. I was reminded that "hurt people hurt people." And I felt free.

Engaging Your Mate: Couples Forgiveness

This next exercise gives you a great opportunity to work with your mate. Before you start, to make things easy, go online and print out this exercise. It is available on our website: www.marriageboot-camp.com. If that's not convenient, don't let it stop you. All you have to do is pass this book back and forth with your partner as you get to the separate "his" and "hers" sections. You will also need some kind of a timer, such as your phone or an egg timer; make sure that you stick to the time limits we've set, as this keeps some semblance of order in this very emotional exercise.

MARRIAGE BOOT CAMP QUICK SCRIPT

If you need help broaching the subject, here is a quick script:

"I've learned so much about bringing the love back to our relationship in *Marriage Boot Camp*, and there is an exercise to help get us back to the closeness we used to have without it turning into an argument. I want that for us, and I think this will help. There's also some great music to listen to as part of this exercise. Would you be willing to take this challenge?

"The Marriage Boot Camp says that a lot of relationships get stuck because bitterness gets pent up in a person's heart, and when that happens it's almost impossible to solve everyday issues. Can I read you the part on forgiveness?" (Go back to pages 250–259 and read them to your mate, up to the Boot Camp Call to Action—Part I.) "In this exercise, we are going to walk through the process of forgiving each other.

"There are some handouts that I've printed out as part of the exercise. We are to keep them facedown for now." (Pass out copies of the handout.) Or say, "There are specific sections for each of us, and we'll just pass the book back and forth." That can be a sharing experience in itself.

"Now they suggest that we sit face-to-face, hold hands, close our eyes, and listen to this song." (Play: "I Miss My Friend" by Darryl Worley.)

"Now we are to go through some questions and talk through our thoughts together. The rules say that when one person is talking, the other person is only listening. I commit to letting you say your piece. Will you also commit to the rules?"

Let them know also that this is *not* conflict resolution. This process will not necessarily resolve any problems; it will simply take some of the fire out of the dispute. Often, we just want to have our pain acknowledged by our mate. You may still have work to do after forgiveness. Think deeply about these questions and discuss:

- What would our relationship be like if we could release all of our past hurts?
- What would our relationship be like if we were able to let go of all ill will toward each other?
- What would our relationship look like if we were able to get what we really wanted from our relationship?
- How would you feel if we could start this relationship over with a clean slate?

This is an opportunity to start over. We can have the relationship we really want if we are willing to give a little and let go of past hurts. Imagine that we could have the moment when we first got together back, that we could have our best friend back.

Now let's move on in this exercise. Sit face-to-face and, holding hands, look into each other's eyes. Make a commitment to stick to the script and the timer and not get into an argument. Men will begin, women will go second, and then men will finish up. Remember, when one person is talking, the other is listening!

Men (Yes, you're first this time!):
Think about the harm that you've committed against your wife. When you have your list in your head, share this by saying:

ELIZABETH AND JIM CARROLL

- "Here is a list of the things I've done to hurt you . . ."
- "If there's anything I left off my list, please tell me . . ."

Let her speak. You should now have a complete list of offenses from both parties. Don't move on until you both agree that this list is complete.

Now you will begin a timed task. Ask your mate how these offenses have made her feel about herself and about you. Allow her to speak everything in her heart for no more than three minutes. Then, with all your heart, look into her eyes and say:

- "I am sorry for all of the pain I have caused you." Look into her eyes and let this register.
- "I am sorry that I haven't always treated you the way you deserve." Look into her eyes and let this register.
- "I'm sorry for all the times I've taken you for granted." Look into her eyes and let this register.
- "Please forgive me so that *you* can be free." Look into her eyes and let this register.

Men, read this next part silently to yourself:
It is now her turn to forgive you. Don't get upset if your mate says she forgives you for something that you don't feel responsible for. Whether an issue is real or perceived, it's real to her. Don't argue. Just allow her to forgive you so she can let it go. Now prompt her to start with her first page or give her this book.

Women (Thank you for your patience):

- Pick one small thing that you need to forgive him for and say, "I forgive you for _____." Fill in the blank.
- Pick something a little bigger and tell him, "I forgive you for _____."
- Now, pick something pretty big and tell him, "I forgive you for _____."
- Now, pick the biggest thing and tell him, "I forgive you for _____."

Ladies, please read this silently and follow the instructions:
Think about anything and everything you *haven't* forgiven. Take a deep breath and hold it in. Hold it for ten to fifteen seconds before you release it or until you are uncomfortable. That's what unforgiveness feels like.

Now count to three; slowly let your breath out, letting go of any and all anger you have toward your mate. Breathe in again and hold it for one, two, three . . . and slowly let your breath out.

If you can, say, "I forgive you for everything."

It's now the wife's turn to apologize. Think about the harm you've committed against your husband. When you have your list in your head, say:

- "Here is a list of the things I've done to hurt you . . ."
- "If there anything I left off my list, please tell me . . ."

Let him speak. You should now have a complete list of offenses. Don't move on until you both agree that this list is complete.

Ladies, this is a timed task. Ask your mate how these offenses have made him feel about himself, and about you. Allow him to speak everything in his heart for no more than three minutes.

Then, with all your heart, look into his eyes and say:

- "I am sorry for all of the pain I have caused you." Look into his eyes and let this register.
- "I am sorry that I haven't always treated you the way you deserve." Look into his eyes and let this register.
- "I'm sorry for all the times I've taken you for granted." Look into his eyes and let this register.
- "Please forgive me so that *you* can be free." Look into his eyes and let this register.

Ladies, read this next part silently to yourself:
It is now his turn to forgive you. Don't get upset if your mate says he forgives you for something that you don't feel responsible for. Whether an issue is real or perceived, it's real to him. Don't argue. Just allow him to forgive you so that he can let it go. Prompt him to start with his second page, or give the book back to your husband.

Men
- Pick one small thing that you need to forgive her for and say, "I forgive you for _____." Fill in the blank.
- Pick something a little bigger and tell her, "I forgive you for _____."
- Now, pick something pretty big and tell her, "I forgive you for _____."

■ Now, pick the biggest thing and tell her, "I forgive you for _____."

Men, please read this silently and follow the instructions:
Think about anything and everything you haven't forgiven. Take a deep breath and hold it in. Hold it for ten to fifteen seconds before you release it or until you are uncomfortable. That's what unforgiveness feels like.

Now count to three; slowly let your breath out, letting go of any and all anger you have toward your mate. Breathe in again and hold it. Count one, two, three . . . and slowly let your breath out.

If you can, say, "I forgive you for everything."

Now stand up and give each other a long hug. Hold on as long as you need to, taking deep, cleansing breaths.

One Last Thing . . .

There is one last thing regarding forgiveness that bears discussion. After forgiveness, a void exists where the hate and anger used to be. This hate and anger have been there so long that it almost feels like a natural part of your life, and it will draw you back if you leave it empty. It is time to fill the void, but this time with love.

Love is *not* a romantic feeling of infatuation, though that may be a part of the experience of love. American philosopher Dallas Willard defines love as "a willing of the greater good for another." Love is an action taken on behalf of another. The Marriage Boot Camp recommends using a blessing as an act of love to begin to fill the void.

BOOT CAMP CALL TO ACTION—PART III

Pray for your mate. If you don't believe in prayer, then make a wish. Pray or wish for him or her to find freedom from all the anger and to find love.

MARRIAGE BOOT CAMP QUICK SCRIPT

Here are some examples of what you might say to release your spouse from anger:

"Lord, I pray that my mate will have complete freedom from all anger and bitterness toward _____, and that love will pour into his/her life with an energizing and joy-filled light."

"My wish for you is that you have complete freedom from all anger and bitterness toward _____ and that love will pour into your life with an energizing and joy-filled light."

Remember to use this tool for the rest of your life. Anger will always try to come back, but you can use this new tool and be free anytime. I challenge you to think of everyone you need to forgive and go through this process over and over until you have released everything.

Richard and Alice's Story Continued

Richard and Alice learned a lot during their experience at Marriage Boot Camp, but going through the forgiveness drill had more impact on their relationship than on the relationships of any of the other attendees. Both Richard and Alice finally made the choice to release each other from the anger and bitterness that they had held against each other and completely forgave each other for the stupid mistakes they had made so many years before. Completely. Richard and Alice were finally free.

Alice also lived with the memory of falling short of her own standards, and she was filled with guilt and self-loathing much of the time. Alice needed to forgive herself.

It was an extremely emotional process for both Richard and Alice, but they left the Marriage Boot Camp hand in hand, freer and happier than they had ever been. The two of them were behaving like teenagers in love and said they had never felt this kind of love before. Even their children could see the difference! The change in Richard and Alice not only affected them but also their children, and their children's children, and potentially, many generations to come.

This is what can happen when you rip the root of bitterness out of your life and make a commitment to dig it up and throw it away every time it sprouts its ugly head. You can get your love back! You can be free from the past! You now have the tools to deal with the pain that comes with a normal, imperfect life.

CONCLUSION

Your past is your past, the present is your now, and the future is what you decide to make of it. If you hold on to past hurts and transgressions in a relationship and let the anger fester, what chance can you possibly have for a happy, healthy marriage? You don't have a chance, and that's the truth.

Sadly, the bad things that happen to us in our lives when we are younger play into how we react and interact with our spouses when we grow up. And without a better understanding of what drives us to lose our tempers, withhold affection, or pick fights with our spouse, we cannot even begin to fix those problems.

The good news is that with this book, you've obtained real tools for communicating, compromising, resolving conflicts, understanding each other's differences, and forgiving each other for the things you've been holding grudges about. It's up to you to work the program and to figure out the best way to apply the skills and techniques to your life. But if you give it one hundred percent, you will get to a much deeper understanding of yourself and your relationship—even if your spouse didn't participate in reading this book with you.

Just because your mate hasn't read the steps of the Marriage Boot Camp program doesn't mean that you can't utilize those tools when you're dealing with conflict. Believe us, if one half of a couple changes the way he or she fights, the other half will notice. Maybe not immediately, but with consistency you'll succeed at changing the way you two fight and find solutions to conflict. Certainly, two heads are better than one, and in Marriage Boot Camp we believe that marriage is not a fifty-fifty proposition but a one hundred–one hundred commitment for life. But if your partner isn't ready to use a self-help guide to save his or her marriage, you can still single-handedly improve your life and your love. With some serious effort on your part, you can slowly turn the tide. You might even find yourself revisiting the idea of reading the book together. Don't give up! Continue to give one hundred percent!

A BLESSING FROM JIM AND ELIZABETH

We want to personally applaud you for working hard for your marriage and family. It's a passion that we share with you. Healthy marriages create healthy families, healthy children, and a healthy society. So we end this book the way we end every Marriage Boot Camp, with the prayer of blessing for your marriage.

May your marriage and all of your relationships be blessed because of the love that you have shown in seeking ways to grow. May your love be patient and kind, without jealousy or pride and without a record of wrongs. May your burdens be lighter for having partners to help you carry them!